NEED ANALYSIS

Tools for the Human Services and Education

Jack McKillip

Applied Social Research Methods Series
Volume 10

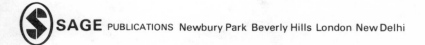

SAGE PUBLICATIONS Newbury Park Beverly Hills London New Delhi

Applied Social Research Methods Series

Series Editor:
LEONARD BICKMAN, Peabody College, Vanderbilt University

Series Associate Editor:
DEBRA ROG, COSMOS Corporation, Washington, D.C.

This series is designed to provide students and practicing professionals in the social sciences with relatively inexpensive softcover textbooks describing the major methods used in applied social research. Each text introduces the reader to the state of the art of that particular method and follows step-by-step procedures in its explanation. Each author describes the theory underlying the method to help the student understand the reasons for undertaking certain tasks. Current research is used to support the author's approach. Examples of utilization in a variety of applied fields, as well as sample exercises, are included in the books to aid in classroom use.

Volumes in this series:

Additional volumes currently in development

NEED ANALYSIS

Tools for the Human Services and Education

Applied Social Research Methods Series
Volume 10

to Mary, of course

Acknowledgments

Thanks to the students in my classes on need analysis who, over the years, have taught me what the topic was all about. Special thanks to Emil Posavac, Richard Hunter, and Carol Lynn Courtney for comments on the manuscript.

For information address:

SAGE Publications, Inc.
2111 West Hillcrest Drive
Newbury Park, California 91320

SAGE Publications Inc.   SAGE Publications Ltd.
275 South Beverly Drive   28 Banner Street
Beverly Hills   London EC1Y 8QE
California 90212   England

SAGE PUBLICATIONS India Pvt. Ltd.
M-32 Market
Greater Kailash I
New Delhi 110 048 India

Printed in the United States of America

Library of Congress Cataloging-in-Publication Data

McKillip, Jack.
  Need analysis for the human services and education.

  (Applied social research methods series ; v. 10)
  Bibliography: p.
  Includes index.
  1. Social surveys. 2. Basic needs. I. Title.
II. Series.
HN29.M369 1986   301'.0723   86-15492
ISBN 0-8039-2647-2
ISBN 0-8039-2648-0 (pbk.)

FIRST PRINTING

CONTENTS

1

Identifying Needs

Needs are value judgments: that a target group has problems that can be solved. Problems are violations of expectancies. Four types of expectations are discussed: normative, felt, expressed, and comparative. Solutions vary in impact, cost, and feasibility. Need analysis involves the identification and evaluation of needs. Need identification is a process of describing problems of a target population and solutions to these problems. Needs assessment evaluates the importance and relevance of the problems and solutions. Constructs of "want" and "demand" are presented and compared to "need."

Need analysis is a tool for decision making in the human services and education. Decisions can be varied, including resource allocation, grant funding, and planning. The following are examples:

- A university division of continuing education must decide how, if at all, to expand its offerings.
- A Department of Mental Health must develop a resource allocation formula.
- A community hospital seeks funding for an adolescent health outreach program.
- A multiservice agency wants to adapt its offerings to attract larger numbers of working class clients.
- A professional organization wants to know what training workshops it should offer at its yearly meetings.

In each of these instances, a decision will be made, a decision to act or not to act. Decisions that can be helped by need analysis start with two judgments: (a) *services available to a population are (or are not) adequate;* and (b) if inadequate, *specific actions will correct the inadequacy.* If services are inadequate and corrective programming is available, there is a need. If services are adequate, there is no need. Sometimes, as with herpes and AIDS, there are no solutions. There are only problems. In these cases, "need" analysis is "problems analysis" and problems are identified and evaluated. Because there are usually many needs, once needs are identified, they must be evaluated so choices can be made among them. This book focuses on gathering, structuring, and presenting information to aid decisions about need.

The next section outlines the steps in need analysis. Subsequent sections define need and discuss aspects of this definition: for example, recognition of problems, identification of solutions, and the role of values. The final section of this chapter presents the constructs of want and of demand and contrasts them with need.

1.1 Steps in Need Analysis

The five steps of need analysis are presented in Table 1.1 and discussed below.

1   *Identify users and uses.* The first step for need analysis, like that for all decision-aiding processes, is to identify the users and uses of the analysis. The literature on use of social research (e.g., Weiss & Bucuvalas, 1980) makes it clear that attention to the users of a study is critical. Neglect at this step leads to unused and unread reports. The users of the analysis are those who will act on the basis of the report. Audiences, who may be affected by the report but will not act on it, also should be included. Often users will not be fully aware of how the analysis will be used. Pitz and McKillip (1984, especially Chapter 4) provide procedures to help users think about how applied research will be used and what kind of information should be gathered. Knowing the uses of the need analysis helps focus on the problems and solutions that can be entertained. For example, knowing that the analysis will form the basis for a community mental health center's application for funding from the state department of alcoholism prescribes the needs that can be identified.[1]

2   *Description of target population and service environment.* The second step in need analysis is description of the target population and the existing service environment. Geographic dispersion, transportation, demographic characteristics of the target population, eligibility restrictions, and service capacity are important. Client analysis, the comparison of those who use services with those who are eligible to use services, is described in Section 4.5. Resource inventories, detailing services available, are described in Chapter 3. The presence of comple-

TABLE 1.1

Steps in Need Analysis

1. Identify USERS and USES of the need analysis.
2. Describe the TARGET POPULATION and the SERVICE ENVIRONMENT.
3. IDENTIFY needs
—Describe PROBLEMS
—Describe SOLUTIONS
4. ASSESS the importance of the needs
5. COMMUNICATE results

mentary and competing agencies affects the solutions that can be considered.

3   *Need identification.* The third step is need identification. Here problems of the target population(s) and possible solutions are described. Usually more than one source of information is used. Identification should include information on expectations for outcomes, on current outcomes, and on the impact and cost of solutions. Attention is not paid to ordering or evaluating the importance of needs at this step (Siegel, Attkisson, & Carson, 1978). Chapters 3-7 present need identification techniques in detail.

4   *Needs assessment.* Once problems and their solutions have been identified, needs are evaluated. Which are most important for the target population? Which are most relevant to the mission and experiences of the sponsoring agency? How are multiple and conflicting indicators to be integrated? Need analysis will be most useful for decision making if identified needs are evaluated against explicit and appropriate criteria. This is the task of needs assessment. The next chapter discusses three models of needs assessment and Chapter 9 provides a detailed application of the decision-making model.

5   *Communication.* Finally, the results of a need identification must be communicated to decision makers, users, and other relevant audiences. The effort that goes into communication should equal that given the other steps of the need analysis. Chapter 10 reviews methods of written and oral communication that will help users understand the need analysis.

In practice, need analysis is an *iterative* and *satisficing* activity: the cycle of decision, data gathering, and data analysis repeats until further cycles are judged unnecessary. Though the description so far implies an orderly and incremental process, this rarely happens. Questions are raised about potential problems and/or solutions; information is gathered and evaluated. Analysis leads to further questions, data gathering, and evaluation. The process ends when those engaged are satisfied that additional information would not be worth the cost of gathering and analysis. Distinctions between identification and assessment are blurred. Analysis may involve multiple identifications and assessments.

1.2 Definition of Need

Judgments of adequacy are not unique to the human services and education. They are made daily by people in every walk of life. A business's decision to move into a new market, an individual's decision to see a doctor, and a senator's efforts to get legislation adopted rest on judgments about need.

A need is the value judgment that *some group has a problem that can be solved*. There are four aspects of this definition:

(1) Recognizing need involves *values*. People with different values will recognize different needs. Further, the person seeing the need and the person experiencing the need may differ. An observer may judge your state of affairs inadequate, even though you yourself experience no dissatisfaction.

(2) A need is possessed by a particular group of people in a certain set of circumstances. A description of the *target population* and its environment is an important part of need analysis.

(3) A *problem* is an inadequate outcome, an outcome that violates expectations. There are many sources of expectations, reflecting different values. For example, students' reading levels can indicate a problem if they do not meet parents', or teachers', or students' expectations. Problems also can be indicated by inadequate process, if there is the expectation that, without action, inadequate outcomes will develop.

(4) Recognition of a need involves a judgment that a *solution* exists for a problem. A problem may have many potential solutions, solutions that vary in the probability of alleviating the problem, and in the cost and the feasibility of implementation. Unfortunately, much of the literature on need analysis focuses more on the recognition of problems than the identification of solutions.

1.3 Identifying Needs

Evaluating needs requires information on the type and the magnitude of problems, and on the cost, impact, and feasibility of solutions. This section summarizes the information required to judge problems and solutions.

Recognizing Problems

Three types of problems are identified by need analyses. First, problems are revealed by comparison of expectations with outcomes. *Discrepancies* are problems. Expectations can be for ideal or maximum outcome levels, such as the goals used to construct UWASIS II (Section 3.3); for minimal outcome levels, such as the poverty level or the ability to read want ads; and for comparative levels, such as the ratio of female to male hourly wage.

A second type of problem afflicts those *at-risk* of developing poor outcomes. At-risk groups possess characteristics that either directly predict poor outcomes or, because of inaction, do so indirectly. Social indicators (Chapter 4) are often chosen because they predict poor outcomes, for example, admissions to mental hospitals or use of welfare. Lack of a relevant skill, as revealed by a training survey (Section 6.4), may lead to poor job performance if action is not taken. Substandard levels of service delivery (Section 5.3) may lead to deaths or suicides if services are not improved.

A third type of problem is what Scriven and Roth (1978) call *maintenance* need. A group with maintenance needs can develop poor outcomes if services presently offered are withdrawn or altered. Need analyses that include cutbacks or cancellation of ongoing programming as an option should measure maintenance needs.

Outcome Expectations

Problems are recognized by comparison with expectations for what can or ought to be. Bradshaw (1972) identifies four types of expectations that support judgments of need. The first is *normative* need, an expectation based on an expert definition of adequate levels of performance or service. Because of their experience and knowledge, experts can provide guidance about what outcomes should be expected and about levels of service required to reach these outcomes. The Joint

Committee on the Accreditation of Hospitals' standards for the operation of community mental health centers (Section 5.3) provide normatively based expectations for services that mental health centers provide. Normative expectations are particularly useful in planning areas in which there is little previous experience. However, because of the dependence on experts, normative expectations can be elitist and can lead to programming that the target population does not use.

Bradshaw's (1972) second type of expectation leads to *felt* need. These are expectations that members of a group have for their own outcomes. Parents' expectations about the appropriate amount of elementary level mathematics instruction or clients' expectations for the behavior of counselors can lead to felt needs. Many training needs assessments (Section 6.4) and much marketing research are based on this type of expectation. Surveys (Chapter 6) and community forums (Section 7.4) provide a ready source of felt needs. Felt needs depend on the insight the target population has into its own problems. If a need for a service is not felt by the target population, it probably will not be used. At the same time, many of the expectations for human service and educational programming are unrealistic.

Expectations for outcomes can be based on the behavior of the target population, called *expressed need*. Expectations are indicated by use of services, for example, waiting lists, enrollment pressure, or high bed occupancy rates. For many planning and budgeting decisions, the litmus test is utilization. If a service will be used, it can be funded. If it is not used, it will not be funded. However, just because a service is used does not mean that the use is appropriate. Because expressed needs rely on use of services that are currently available, they can produce solutions that continue the status quo.

The final expectation that Bradshaw (1972) decribes is *comparative* need. These expectations are based on the performance of a group other than the target population. If a group (or an individual) uses a service less than another or scores above or below the average of the population on a performance measure, it has a problem. For example, Warheit and Bell (1983) classified an individual as needing mental health services if, by test scores, he was more depressed than 84% of a study sample. Comparisons allow extrapolations from information already available. Comparative expectations depend on the similarity of the comparison group and the target population and can neglect unique characteristics that invalidate generalizations.

Each of the expectations that Bradshaw (1972) discusses has strong points and weaknesses. None is appropriate for all decision situations. Specific need identification techniques reviewed in Chapters 3-7 emphasize one or the other of these expectations. Because of the underlying expectations, a combination of techniques will present a less biased picture of the needs of a population. Criteria for choosing among techniques are discussed in Chapter 8.

Identifying Solutions

Identification of problems is much better understood in the human services and education than identification of solutions. This is due, in part, to the modest investments made in program evaluation. Nothing would aid the identification of solutions more than the existence of hard-headed impact assessment of current programming. This section reviews three criteria for evaluating solutions: Cost, impact, and feasibility.

Cost analysis. The first step in estimating costs is selecting a time frame. Usually a one-year period is appropriate.[2] Cost of equipment and facilities that have a longer life than this period should be adjusted accordingly. The next step is listing the resources necessary for the solution to operate during the period. Resources can be estimated from comparable efforts currently under way or from previous experience with the intervention. Resources (Levin, 1983) include the following:

- personnel, including volunteers
- facilities, even if the program will use current agency space
- equipment, even if shared with other programs
- materials and supplies
- client costs, including transportation and fees
- others, including utilities, insurance, and administrative overhead

The third step in cost analysis is determining the cost of each of the resources. If program budgets are consulted for this information, some resources may not be covered, because costs might have been borne in a different year or by a different account. The following are examples of methods for determining costs:

Personnel	Salary (plus fringe benefits) for paid staff; estimate the value of volunteers by the salaries that would need to be paid to accomplish the work done by the volunteers.
Facilities	Rent (currently paid or estimated from that charged for similar space). Current market rates should be used even if the agency has facilities that are already paid for. Programs that use only part of a building or office can be assigned a cost on a per-square-foot basis. If a program uses 40% of the area of an office, the facility costs are 40% of the rent for the office. Renovations should be depreciated over the anticipated life of the program.
Equipment	Rental or lease cost, or depreciate cost over the expected life of the equipment. If equipment is shared, cost may be divided by the amount the equipment is used. Equipment costs can also be assigned on a per-square-foot basis.
Material and supplies	Cost of materials actually used (not budgeted) for the project.
Client costs	Transportation figured at the travel reimbursement rate for staff; fees actually paid by clients.
Other	Figured on actual expenses or on a per-square-foot basis.

Finally, the cost of individual resources are added to determine the overall cost of the proposed solution.

Impact. Impacts are much more difficult to measure than costs,[3] because reliable and valid information is rarely available. When it is available, it should be consulted. In addition, because impacts are usually multiple and not all in the same direction, a method must be found to aggregate these impacts. (They cannot simply be added as are costs! See Chapter 9.) Sometimes the only evidence for impact will be intuition and hope. In the more usual cases in which there is some experience and literature available, a solution is to submit all this information to an expert panel (e.g., delphi panel, Section 7.3). When solutions to the same problem are being compared, experts might rate solutions on the extent to which the problem is alleviated, from not at all (0) to the extent to which alleviation is possible (10). If solutions to different problems are to be compared, experts might judge the overall benefit of each to the target population.

Feasibility. Given the state of knowledge, feasibility of implementation (Datta, 1978) is often more important for judging solutions than is impact. Besides cost, implementation is affected by the time needed to set up the proposed solution, the time taken to deliver the solution, and the fit of the solution within the structure and environment of the agency. Some solutions require rigid adherence to a model, others can easily be adapted to the staffing and physical resources available. Some solutions will appeal to the staff and to the clientele currently served by the agency, other programs will not interest current clients but will attract a new clientele, and still other programs may be viewed hostilely by both staff and clients. Some solutions will require reorganization of staff structure and routine (these will be the most difficult to implement). Each aspect of a proposed solution should be examined to judge the feasibility of a proposed solution. Assessment by an expert panel (as described above) or a more formal analysis (see Chapter 9) may be used to integrate this information. The best solution for a problem has low cost, high impact, and is feasible for the agency to implement.

1.4 Role of Values in Determining Need

Defining need as a judgment points out how important values are in need analysis, both in identification and evaluation. Values are reflected in expectations for outcomes that underlie problem recognition. Experts have expectations different from those of a target population (see Exhibit 6.2). Experts may take a broader view but often overemphasize problems. The expectations of the target population are critical to use of the services but may be self-serving and unrealistic. Examination of actual patterns of use often presumes the adequacy of the status quo. Finally, expectations based on the experiences of groups other than the target population assume comparability of the groups.

Identification of solutions also involves value judgments. The mission statement of an agency and the skills of its personnel lead to specific types of programming. If a problem cannot be thought of in a way that allows application of the finite set of solutions in the agency's repertoire, it will not become a need. Alcohol abuse counselors rarely do manpower training and therapists usually are not qualified as financial advisers. Current or previously tried solutions often persist, even in the face of demonstrated lack of impact.

Once identified, the evaluation of needs requires that values be incorporated into analysis. Different models of needs assessment reflect different value orientations (see Chapter 2). Chapter 9 reviews in detail a method of incorporating the values of the users of the need analysis into the evaluation of needs.

The analysis of need cannot be value free; values are central to the recognition and evaluation of needs. Need analyses are done better if the value choices involved are made explicit, rather than left implicit.

1.5 Wants and Demands

It is useful to compare the definition of need used here with other popular terms: wants and demands.[4]

By far the most widely used alternative to need is *want*: something people are willing to pay for.[5] Most businesses, and many human service and education providers, seek to satisfy people's wants by providing goods and services that people are willing to trade something of value for. When judging whether the current mix of products and services is adequate (i.e., whether wants exist), the primary question is: "Will the target population pay for some additional product or service?"

The focus of wants is on utilization. If a product does not sell, it is not wanted. The credibility given to wants comes from a marketplace in which individuals freely choose how to spend their resources. The question of whether a wanted service "solves a problem" is rarely raised.

A drawback for use of wants in human services and education is that competitive markets for programs often do not exist. Client costs are subsidized and the ability of consumers to make judgments in their own best interests is often questioned. Nevertheless indicators of wants can be relevant for need analysis.

In political arenas, the term used most frequently is *demand*: something people are willing to march for. Political decision makers had been making judgments of adequacy long before the advent of social indicators or survey research, mostly based on demands made by their constituencies. Demands are heard through letters, petitions, public hearings, election outcomes, street demonstrations, and campaign contributions.

Demands differ from wants because the target population, rather than a service provider, usually originates and presents a demand. It is probably because of the absence of a market that human service and educational needs are frequently identified by politically-oriented techniques.

Often, need involves the recognition of a problem by observers. A need has a more dispassionate quality than a demand and, because of this, is more popular with planners and academic researchers than with politicians. "Objective" or rational indicators of need are frequently cited as alternatives to political assessments. However, the person that another believes to be in need may neither recognize a problem nor use its solution. Many of the more familiar techniques of need identification share this drawback: They are aimed at helping *observers* identify problems that a target population has.

EXERCISES

1. Sketch goals for a high school birth control education program from the perspectives of students, of teachers, and of parents. What aspects of such a program are affected by the values of these three groups?

2. Recent reports on the problems of primary and secondary education have compared performance of U.S. students on standardized mathematical tests with that of students in other developed countries. How would this type of data fit in Bradshaw's categories of need? What other types of information could be used to identify educational needs?

3. Examine the editorial page of today's paper. Categorize the issues raised there as wants, demands, or needs. Which category is the most popular? Why?

NOTES

1. Sometimes users of a need analysis feel that they cannot be explicit about how the analysis will used. This is unfortunate because it greatly decreases the likelihood of their receiving a usable product.

2. Costs borne over different years can complicate analysis because future costs must be discounted for comparison to present costs. Levin (1983) and Thompson (1980) present useful introductions to cost analysis.

3. Posavac and Carey's (1985) text on program evaluation provides a useful introduction.

4. Distinctions among needs, wants, and demands were brought to my attention by Dr. Richard Hunter.

5. "Pay" need not be understood monetarily, but more broadly in terms of some valued commodity, for example, time.

2

Evaluating Needs:
Models and Examples

Three models of needs assessment are described along with examples of each. The discrepancy model evaluates gaps between expectations of experts and the outcomes of the target population. The marketing model evaluates the fit between the consumer's desires and the ability of agencies to deliver services. The decision-making model evaluates identified needs in light of the values and interests of those who will use the need analysis, the decision makers. All models of need analyses presume that a decision will be made about competing needs. The relationship between need analysis, program evaluation, and decision making is discussed.

2.1 Why Analyze Needs?

Need analyses are used for the following:

- *advocacy* in grant preparation or other funding requests
- *budgeting* to set funding priorities
- *description* for understanding, for academic theses or publications
- *evaluation* as part of both formative and summative studies of an intervention
- *planning* for decision making about program implementation
- *testimony* to create community awareness, to show action on a problem, to satisfy a legislative mandate

Whatever the combination of uses, the role of a systematic analysis of need is the *reduction of uncertainty.* Someone, either the person commissioning the study or some group important to this person, is uncertain about what, if any, programming should be added or reduced. Need analysis seeks to reduce this uncertainty.

In need identification, uncertainty concerns the problems of a target population and solutions available for these problems. The techniques described in Chapters 3-7 can reduce uncertainty by gathering information about the needs of the target population. In needs assessment, uncertainty concerns the best actions (or nonactions) to be taken to meet these needs. Models of needs assessment define "best" in different ways, by maximizing different values. The discrepancy model maximizes normative or experts' values. The marketing model maximizes consumers' values. The decision-making model, presented in detail in Chapter 9, maximizes the values of those who will use the results of the need analysis, the decision makers.

2.2 Models of Needs Assessment

Needs assessment is the process of evaluating the problems and solutions identified for a target population. Assessing needs moves beyond the information gathering of need identification, requiring evaluative judgments about problems and their solutions. This section describes three models of needs assessment and provides an example of each. The *discrepancy model* is the most straightforward and widely used, especially in education. The *marketing model* is new to the human services and education, but will probably gain favor with continued budget restrictions and increased emphasis on the wants of consumers. The *decision-making model* emphasizes utilization of the need analysis itself by attending to the values and information needs of decision makers.

Discrepancy Model

The discrepancy or gap model is the most widely used approach to needs assessment (e.g., Kaufman & English, 1979). The model emphasizes normative expectations and involves three phases:

(1) goal setting, identifying what ought to be;
(2) performance measurement, determining what is;
(3) discrepancy identification, ordering differences between what ought to be and what is.

Witkin (1977) presents a good overview of the discrepancy model and Exhibit 2.1 presents a detailed example.

During the goal-setting phase performance expectations are derived. Typically, an expert group is surveyed concerning dimensions of desirable performance in the area of the need analysis. "Desirable" performance may reflect necessary or minimal skills required for a task, useful skills, or a utopian wish. Performance expectations, or goals, are obtained for each of the performance dimensions, from the original or a second group of experts. Performance expectations are indicators of what ought to be. As examples, managers may be surveyed about possible inservice areas for new employees; teachers might be asked about arithmetic performance levels for grade school graduation; or the data processing personnel might be asked about computer hardware additions.

The second step in the analysis is performance measurement, that is, determining what is. Actual outcomes are determined for the target population on each of the performance dimensions. This is often done by survey, although most of the need identification techniques described in Chapters 3 to 7 can be used.

The third step of analysis is discrepancy identification; gaps are computed between what is and what ought to be. "Need" is indicated where measured performance is lower than desired levels. Often, needs are ordered by the size of the gap between performance and goal, larger gaps indicate greater needs. Programming begins in the area of the largest performance gap. As an alternative, after gaps are determined, an expert panel (either the original or a new one) is consulted. The panel rates the importance of the gaps that have been identified. Ratings reveal need: The most important gap is the most important need, and so on.

The discrepancy model usually does not distinguish the recognition of problems from the choice of solutions. Problems are identified with specific solutions in mind, as in the training survey discussed in Section 6.4, or solution identification takes place after a problem is selected for intervention.

The discrepancy model has been adapted to many need analysis situations. A delphi panel (Moore, 1987; Section 7.3) can be used to get consensus among judges. Because of its dependence on experts for identification and assessment of need, the discrepancy model is sometimes seen as elitist.

(2) *Marketing Model*

Some writers (e.g., Marti-Costa & Serrano-Garcia, 1983; Nickens, Purga, & Noriega, 1980) define needs assessment as a feedback process used by organizations to learn about and to adapt to the needs of their client populations. This is not a wholly altruistic process, but "is done by an organization . . . on its own behalf" (Broskowski, 1983, p. 76). Need analysis is a means of organizational survival and growth.

Exhibit 2.1
Assessing Needs of Married Students

Flores (1975) sought to determine service needs of a married student population. On the basis of a literature review and publications of professional organizations, 51 areas of student support and development were studied. After consultation with married students and student personnel professionals, 24 outcome criteria were selected to cover support and development areas, e.g.:

- basic necessities for clothing, food, shelter, and transportation are met;
- after college debts incurred or to be incurred can be paid off with 10% or less of prospective annual income.

Six active student personnel professionals rated desired levels for each of the 24 critieria. Desirable levels were the minimum percentage of students who had to be satisfied for the expert to consider outcomes acceptable (what ought to be). Performance expectations ranged from 74% to 93% satisfied.

A large random sample of married students at two universities were surveyed concerning their personal satisfaction on each of the 24 outcome criteria. Obtained satisfaction levels were the measure of performance (what is).

Discrepancies were identified. Criteria that had measured satisfaction levels lower than the minimum levels indicated as acceptable by the expert panel are given in Table 2.1. The largest gap was in routine consideration given to married students by the college. Need in this area was much greater than, for example, in the area of child care.

Kotler (1982) developed this need-analysis-as-feedback perspective by extending marketing principles from the private to the public sector. The marketing model provides a means of planning for a total organization, covering issues beyond need analysis. The marketing perspective can contribute useful ideas to need analysis.

According to Kotler (1982, p. 37):

A marketing orientation holds that the main task of an organization is to determine the needs and wants of the target markets and to satisfy them through the design, communication, pricing and delivery of appropriate and competitively viable products and services.

TABLE 2.1
Discrepancies in Outcome Criteria Reflecting Needs
of Married Student Housing Residents

Outcome Criteria	Gap between Expert Expectations and Student Satisfaction
The college in its routine recognizes and gives consideration to married students and their families.	17
Student and family enjoy an ample volume of group activity and involvement.	14
A sense of affiliation with the college and community exists, and the family is accepted by at least one specific group within the college or community.	13
Sources of supplementary income available to the student and his or her spouse are sufficient to maintain family support.	10
At the time of entrance, the student possessed crucial information concerning the college's expectations of and opportunities provided for students.	9
Those about to seek career employment have information about job availability and job seeking procedures.	5
Arrangements for child care are affordable, convenient, and contributory to the child's (children's) development.	3

Adapted from Flores (1975).

Central to the marketing orientation is the notion of exchange. Organizations obtain the resources they need by offering something of value to resource owners. Need analysis is a process of identifying and choosing among services for which target populations are willing to trade something the agency values. Needs are wants. Exchanges are not restricted to money. Client time and participation are often crucial in human services and education because they lead to (third-party) payments from parents, government agencies, and foundations.

A marketing strategy of need analysis has three components:

(1) selection of the target population, those actually or potentially eligible for the service and able to make the necessary exchanges;

(2) choice of competitive position, distinguishing the agency's services from those offered by other agencies and providers; and

(3) development of an effective marketing mix, selecting a range and quality of services that will maximize utilization by the target population.

Strategic decisions can result from (a) a product portfolio analysis; and (b) a product/market expansion analysis. In the former, existing products are categorized by acceptance (i.e., use) by the target population and by attractiveness or growth potential of this population. Attractive markets are those increasing in size and in ability (perhaps due to government subsidy) to make exchanges. Accepted services that target attractive and growing markets are needed. Exhibit 2.2 provides an example of such an analysis.

Product/market expansion analysis examines the addition of new services or the expansion into new markets that will maximize exchanges by the target population. Organizations choose among offering new services, expanding to new markets, or a combination of these.

That the marketing model can be of value for organizational planning is probable, whether it would be useful as part of a need analysis is less sure. As the portfolio analysis example makes clear (Exhibit 2.2), a marketing approach defines the needs of the target population by the union of the capabilities of an organization (i.e., the solutions they are good at) and the expressed choices of the target populations. For the marketing model, need is a desire of the target population to make exchanges for a service that the agency can provide. A problem is not so much a deficit in performance as an expectation of the target group of enjoyment. Solutions are services nearly or already within the capabilities and expertise of the agency.

The marketing model leads to need analyses that are responsive to the desires of the target population. Both the discrepancy and the marketing models incorporate measurements of the target population. In the former, the performance dimensions measured are determined by experts. In the latter, dimensions are more likely to be determined by the target population itself.

Exhibit 2.2
Planning for University Offerings

Newbould (1980) illustrated use of a product portfolio matrix to analyze master degree programs offered by three large midwestern state universities. A version of this matrix is shown in Table 2.2.

The "Market Growth Rate" dimension is a measure of the attractiveness of the target population. "Market Share Dominance" is a measure of the acceptance of the university's services. Indicators appropriate for

TABLE 2.2
Product Portfolio Analysis Matrix

| | | Market Share Dominance | |
		High	Low
	High	Stars	Problem Children
Market Growth Rate			
	Low	Cash Cows	Dogs

these dimensions depend on the purposes of the analysis and the mission of the organization.

The cell in Table 2.2 occupied by a particular service has implications for decisions about that service. "Stars" are programs of high acceptance with growing markets. These have the potential for the agency to earn increased exchanges. Stars, however, may require additional resources to realize their potential. "Cash cows" are accepted programs serving markets that are not growing. Expansion of these programs will not lead to as productive increases in exchanges as with stars. Cash cows provide organizations with resources for expansion in other areas. *Problem children* are services that are not well accepted by growing markets. Some of these services might be expanded in the hope of moving them into the star category. *Dogs* are services that are neither well accepted nor serve an attractive target population. These services may be cut back to provide resources to expand stars or to improve the acceptance of problem children.

In Newbould's analysis, growth rate was dichotomized at a projected enrollment increase of 5% over next three years. Less than a 5% projected growth was classified as low and more than 5% was classified as high. Market share dominance was dichotomized at enrollment of 125% of the (next) largest competitor. A masters program that enrolled less than 125% of the largest other program of its kind at one of the studied schools was classified as low on market share dominance; those in which enrollment was 125% or greater were classified as high. In each case the break points were arbitrary, but reasonable.

Table 2.3 shows Newbould's classification of the professional master degree programs from two of the universities.

TABLE 2.3
Portfolio Analysis Matrix,
Adapted from Newbould (1980)

Market Share Dominance
University A

	High	Low
High		Business Music Physical Ed
Low		Education Engineering

Market Growth Rate

University B

	High	Low
High	Music Physical Ed	Business
Low	Education	Engineering

University A has the more difficult, and probably less typical distribution: no stars or cash cows. University B has more balance, having at least one program in each of the matrix cells. In both cases, it may be advantageous to release resources from the dogs to expand a star or to increase the quality of a problem child.

Decision-Making Model

The decision-making model is an adaptation of multiattribute utility analysis (MAUA) (Keeney & Riaffa, 1976) to problems of modeling and synthesis in applied research (Edwards & Newman, 1982; Pitz & McKillip, 1984). Use of the model, reviewed in more detail in Chapter 9, is based on reliable findings from research on utilization, decision making, and applied methodology:

(1) Results of applied research are more likely to be used if they focus on the information needs and values of potential users of the research (Weiss & Bucuvalas, 1980).

(2) Decision makers show biases in judgment when confronted with complex, multidimensional information, such as that resulting from need identification (Kahneman, Slovic, & Tversky, 1982). Biases reflect attempts to simplify the decision problem. They are less apparent when judgments are simplified.

(3) No single indicator nor criterion measures a construct perfectly. Multiple indicators of need are more likely than single indicators to present an accurate measurement of a construct (Cook & Campbell, 1979).

The decision-making model has three stages: problem modeling, quantification, and synthesis. In the modeling stage, need identification takes place. The decision problem is conceptualized by options and decision attributes. Options are the choices confronting the decision maker. Attributes are the measurements gathered for the need identification. Attributes may be the results of social indicator analysis, a key informant's survey, and an analysis of the cost of program implementation. Each option is measured on each attribute.

During the quantification stage, measurements contained in the need identification are transformed to reflect the decision makers' values and interests. First, raw measurements are transformed into utilities. The utility of a measurement is the seriousness of need the decision maker attaches to the particular attribute score.[1] Second, the decision maker's values and interests are quantified by assigning each attribute a weight. These weights reflect the decision makers' assessment of how important the source of information is to the decision, given the other sources available and the range of scores found on the measure.

The final step in the assessment is synthesis. It provides an index that orders options on need. This index also gives information on the relative standing of these needs. The overall need index is computed by multiplying weights and utilities, and summing the products across attributes. The biggest need is the option with the highest index.

Exhibit 2.3 provides an example of the use of the decision-making model. It can explicitly include outcome expectations, actual performance measures, and characterisitcs of solutions.

The decision-making model is distinguished from the discrepancy and marketing models because values and their role in the need analysis are made explicit. The model is generally implemented using the values of a decision maker,[2] but the values of others, including those of the reseacher, can be used instead. A disadvantage of this model is its added complexity.

Exhibit 2.3
Choosing Continuing Education Classes

Pitz and McKillip (1984) use the example of a Director of Continuing Education deciding which courses need to be offered in an upcoming term. The director identified seven courses as options: aerobics, art history, computers, guitar, photography, weaving, and welding. The purpose of the need analysis was to help the director choose among these options based on fixed types of information (attributes): previous enrollment, its relevance for the next enrollment period (a measure of uncertainty), results of a survey of community residents about awareness and interest in the courses, previous student ratings of the courses, and previous student ratings of instructors who would teach the courses. The decision model from the need identification phase is shown in Table 2.4. The enrollment, survey, and rating attributes were obtained from records of previous courses and from a special survey of the community served by the university. For example, the previous aerobics class enrolled 45 students. These students rated the class as 4.2 on a five-point scale and rated the instructor as 4.5 on a five-point scale. It was found that 24% of the respondents to the community survey were aware of the class and 8% were interested in taking it. The attribute of relevance of the enrollment information was the director's subjective judgment of how accurately previous enrollment would predict future enrollment on a scale from 0 to 10. For aerobics, the director was relatively uncertain about the accuracy of the previous enrollment data.

Table 2.5 shows the decision model with weights and with utilities replacing the raw mesurements of Table 2.4. Weights are scaled to sum to 1, indicating the importance or relevance of each attribute for the choice of courses. Weights reflect the director's values. Together, student ratings of the course and community interest in the course account for more than 2/3 of the decision (i.e., .44 + .24 = .68). Options that score well on these attributes are likely to be needed. The utility values in Table 2.5 also reflect the director's values. For example, after some point, enrollment increases cause more problems than benefits. Because of these problems, the computer class was assigned a utility value lower than might be expected based on its raw enrollment score. The final column of Table 2.5 shows the Need Index. The top four

TABLE 2.4
Choosing Continuing Education Courses, Raw Measures

Courses	Enrollment	Relevance of Enrollment	Attributes Community Survey Awareness	Interest	Student Ratings Class	Instructor
Aerobics	45	4	24%	8%	4.2	4.5
Art History	12	9	8%	6%	4.7	4.0
Computers	120	8	38%	35%	4.1	3.5
Guitar	35	8	25%	26%	3.9	4.2
Photography	76	7	32%	12%	4.5	4.6
Weaving	11	7	14%	6%	4.8	4.9
Welding	38	9	28%	15%	4.6	3.5

classes (most needed) were computers, photography, welding, and weaving. Differences among these four courses equal differences among the bottom three.

2.3 Need Analysis, Program Evaluation, and Decision Making

Need analysis and program evaluation have distinct roles to play in planning and managing human service and educational programs. Program evaluations address questions about the past: "What was done?" and "What was it worth?" Need analyses address questions about the future: "What should be done?" Need analysis puts in perspective problems confronting a target population, services available to it, and actions that might be taken.

The procedures presume each other. To evaluate solutions, impacts must be gauged. Estimates of impact require that program evaluations have been done. Without program evaluation, need analysis becomes problem analysis, pointing to deficits but not giving guidance about intervention strategies. Similarly, program evaluation depends on need analysis. If the worth of a program is to be judged, the extent that the program addressed the needs of participants must be gauged. Without need analysis programs cannot be evaluated, they can only be described.

As discussed in these first two chapters, need analysis is an aid to decision making. Need analysis helps decision making by clarifying what and how important needs are. It presumes that choices will be made among competing alternatives. Decision making involves the

TABLE 2.5
Choosing Continuing Education Courses, Transformed Need Measures and Need Index

Courses (weights)	Enrollment (.10)	Relevance of Enrollment (.04)	Attributes Community Survey Awareness (.06)	Interest (.24)	Student Ratings Class (.44)	Instructor (.12)	Need Index N_i
Aerobics	.28	.40	.75	.23	.60	.75	.50
Art History	.02	.90	.23	.09	.85	.50	.51
Computers	.61	.80	.98	.94	.55	.25	.65
Guitar	.21	.80	.77	.79	.45	.60	.56
Photography	.46	.70	.89	.42	.75	.80	.65
Weaving	.02	.70	.50	.09	.90	.95	.60
Welding	.23	.90	.83	.53	.80	.25	.62

actual choice among alternatives. Although analysis can gather and evaluate information about problems and solutions, it is not a substitute for decision making.

EXERCISES

1. Examine recent media reports about solutions to a social problem, for example, child abuse, elder abuse, and homelessness. What models of needs assessment do these reports emphasize? What do these models tell you about the values of those doing the reporting?

2. Which of Bradshaw's needs (normative, felt, expressed, or comparative) are most consistent with the discrepancy model of needs assessment? The marketing model? The decision-making model?

3. Imagine that you are a volunteer board member of the local United Way. Which of the models of needs assessment would appeal to you most? Why? Would your reactions differ if you were dean of a social work school at a private university?

NOTES

1. In more traditional applications, "seriousness" is translated "preference."

2. Multiple decision makers can be incorporated into the model. See Pitz & McKillip (1984).

3

Resource Inventory

Resource inventories describe the services available to a target population and reveal gaps in services. A resource inventory may point to underutilized services and may help agencies and funding bodies avoid launching services and programs where there is already a good deal of competition. However, by itself a resource inventory cannot indicate need. The collection of service information by type of provider and service and by capacity will make the resource inventory more useful.

Identifying needs presumes knowledge of the target population(s) and the services available to it. If this information is not in hand, it should be collected at the beginning of a need analysis. This chapter describes development of a resource inventory and the next details description of a target population.

A resource inventory is a compilation of the services available to one or more target groups, usually in a specific geographical area. The basic question addressed by a resource inventory is "Who is doing what for whom?" It provides a community overview, listing, at least, services available to the target population. Additional information might include description of the agencies and conditions under which the programs are available and descriptions of the types and capacity of services offered. Resource inventories usually result from a survey of service providers (for use of surveys in need analysis see Chapter 6 and Fowler, 1984). Exhibit 3.1 presents an example of a resource inventory.

Resource inventories are usually compiled by agencies with an areawide planning responsibility, for example, local United Way board. An inventory should be consulted whenever such an agency is asked to help fund expanded services.

Empty cells in Table 3.1 indicate combinations of services and treatment groups that were not available in the county. Well-populated cells indicated target group/service combinations in which competition may be fierce. Yet exactly what an empty cell or a well-populated cell indicates cannot be judged from this inventory alone. Additional information on actual or potential demand is required. Note that there are eligibility requirements for some target group/service combinations.

Exhibit 3.1
Country-wide Resource Inventory

Fitzgerald and Cutler (1983) developed an inventory of human services for Jackson County, Illinois. Face-to-face interviews were conducted with directors of 57 agencies covering 27 services funded by the local United Way and by the county mental health taxing body. Fifteen categories of clients were studied. Table 3.1 presents part of a service matrix for four of the services to the adult age group. This group included five of the client categories: alcoholic, drug abuser, mentally ill, developmentally disabled, and general population. The numbers in this table identify agencies and were coded to a service directory. The service directory gave a full description of the agency, its services, hours, and rates.

3.1 Who Is Providing Services?

Service providers usually can be classified by geographical area served and by organizational setting. Subregion analysis is often important. For example, if planning a countywide inventory, service providers might be categorized by political subdivision, educational district, or police district. Generally, the smaller the subregion, the more likely it is that a provider's clients will come from the subregion. Information on who and where services are provided is very important to understanding the services available to a target population.

Though the specific agency that a provider represents is important (as in Exhibit 3.1), categories of agencies are also useful. Are only publicly supported agencies to be involved, or are private agencies and private practitioners to be included? The broader the sample the more realistic the view of the services, especially if a purpose of the inventory is to measure capacity to render particular services. If the number of any type of provider is large, sampling may be necessary (Fowler, 1984).

An important part of developing a resource inventory is to identify a specific person in each agency to supply information. If face-to-face or telephone interviews are to be used, this person should receive the questions enough ahead of time to be able to gather the information desired.

TABLE 3.1
Adult Age Group Service Matrix (partial)

	Primary Target Groups				
	Alcoholic	Drug Abuser	Mentally Ill	Developmentally Disabled	General Population
Supportive and Protective Services					
Legal: provide legal consultation and representation		57[b]	55[d]	14, 18, 38	21, 23, 26, 31, 37, 38, 55[d], 56
Food and shelter: provide or assist in obtaining food or shelter	19, 22, 51	19, 22, 51	10, 19, 22, 51, 55[d]	10, 22, 39	4, 10, 17, 21, 21[a], 23, 24, 30, 34[b], 36, 42, 51, 55[d], 56
Education/Training					
General education: provide education in a variety of topic areas			52	52	8, 21, 27, 32, 42, 48, 52
Vocational education: provide training in a skill or trade to be pursued as a career	13, 16	13, 16	13, 16, 25, 52, 55[d]	13, 14, 16, 18, 25, 52	8, 15, 16, 18, 27, 38, 40[d], 42, 47, 48, 52, 55[d]

NOTE: Numbers in matrix are agency identifications. Key: a = animals; b = criminal offenders only; c = veterans only; d = females only; e = males only.

3.2 What Services Are Provided?

A resource inventory focuses on services and programs available. Careful attention must be paid to choosing and defining services. Service categories should

- be mutually exclusive;
- correspond to state and federal categorical grant requirements;
- be locally meaningful.

Three approaches have been used to develop categories: service typology, client functioning, and eligibility requirements.

3.3 UWASIS II Service Typology

Probably the most widely used typology of human services is that developed by the United Way of America: United Way of America Services Identification System II (UWASIS II; Sumariwalla, 1976). UWASIS II is a system "for identifying, classifying and defining individual, organized human endeavors in relation to major goals of society" (p. 7). There are eight general goals that form the core of the system:

(1) optimal income security and economic opportunity
(2) optimal health
(3) optimal provision of basic material needs
(4) optimal opportunity for the acquisition of knowledge and skills
(5) optimal environmental quality
(6) optimal individual and collective safety
(7) optimal social functioning
(8) optimal assurance of the support and effectiveness of services, through organized action

Each goal is divided into "service systems," major subgroupings of services designed to promote the particular goal. Each service system, in turn, contains one or more services. Services are made up of one or more programs. A program is a group of activities having a particular, narrow objective that can function on its own. UWASIS II is a hierarchical organization of goals and services that covers 587 nonoverlapping programs. Table 3.2 gives an example of this organization.

TABLE 3.2
Example of UWASIS II Goal-to-Program Organization

Goal:	7. Optimal Social Functioning
Service System:	7.1 Individual and Family Life Service System
Service:	7.1.03 Family Supplementing Service
Program:	7.1.03.03 Respite Care: a program designed to provide a brief period of (usually more than 24 hours) relief or rest to individuals who need it and who do not possess the wherewithal to make independent arrangements to take care of their dependents.

Using UWASIS II, a comprehensive resource inventory could be developed for all or part of the spectrum of human services. Besides its use for needs assessment, UWASIS II includes service delivery indicators that are useful for evaluation. For the respite care program of Table 3.2, service delivery indicators are:

(1) number of children and adults receiving respite care
(2) number of individuals receiving relief, rest or respite
(3) days of respite care provided.

3.4 Level of Functioning

One problem with UWASIS II is its emphasis on comprehensiveness, but not continuity, of services. A different approach to selection and categorization of services and programs for a resource inventory is suggested by Carter and Newman (1976; Newman & Rinkus, 1978). This approach uses a problem rather than a solution focus to categorizing services. Traditional diagnostic categories similar to those included in Exhibit 3.1 are supplemented with assessments of social/vocational competence (level of functioning) to describe and communicate the degree of client impairment. Table 3.3 shows a level of functioning scale used by the State of Illinois Department of Mental Health and Developmental Disabilities. The scale is designed to cover a wide range of diagnostic categories and each level is behaviorally based.

Services can be grouped according to the level of functioning of the clients they are meant to serve. For alcoholics, Level II services might include a detoxification center, Level IV and V services might be group therapy, and Level IX services might be prevention programming. Continuity of services can be gauged through this vertical type of analysis. Gaps in service levels for a client group are at-risk indicators.

TABLE 3.3
Level of Functioning Scale (Symptom Distress)
Adult Mentally Ill and Drug Abusers, Region 5,
Illinois Department of Mental Health and
Developmental Disabilities

Dysfunctional

Level I
Dysfunctional in all areas and is almost totally dependent upon others to provide supportive, protective environment. Unable to provide for basic personal self-care.

Level II
Symptoms are so severe as to render person incapable of functioning independently. Behavior unpredictable. Symptom severity requires protective surroundings. May hear voices and/or demonstrate delusional thinking.

Level III
Symptoms are so severe as to require almost constant supervision. May be actively suicidal or delusional. Behavior likely unpredictable. Probably experiencing crises involving outside agencies. Community involvement should be restricted. May be living in ordinary social unit, but most psychiatric hospital discharges functioning at higher level.

Level IV
Symptoms require consistent intervention, likely with psychotropic medication. Stressful situations result in exacerbation of symptoms. May exhibit symptoms of chronic psychiatric disorders. Symptoms decrease with therapeutic intervention but likely to recur if intervention is withdrawn.

Functional

Level V
Low stress tolerance, moderate-to-severe symptom distress making regular therapeutic intervention advisable. If situation crisis, symptoms sufficiently severe as to effect other areas of functioning and may lead to withdrawal from normal social contacts. Most people around the person would be aware of symptoms.

Level VI
Symptoms' presence and severity are probably sufficient to be both noticeable and somewhat disconcerting to the individual and/or to those around him or her in daily contact. Symptoms should not prevent person from functioning in work or personal relationships. Regular therapeutic intervention probably important to improve level of functioning.

Level VII
Symptoms recur sufficiently frequently to maintain reliance on regular therapeutic intervention. Those around individual may not be aware of symptoms. Someone who is functioning quite well in all areas but is dependent upon regular therapeutic or pharmacological intervention to maintain level of functioning.

Level VIII
Functioning well in all areas with little evidence of distress. May be former client who makes periodic contact for reassurance or support in infrequent crisis. Occasional recurrence of symptoms justifies maintenance of some very limited contact with treatment resource. Availability of occasional supportive contact may help to maintain level of functioning.

Level IX
Functioning well in all areas with no treatment contact recommended.

NOTE: Full scale covers four areas: personal self-care, social, vocational/educational, and symptom distress.

Alcoholics in the community may need a service intermediate between detoxification and group therapy, i. e. Level III. Gaps may also lead to over-(or under-) utilization at other levels.

3.5 Eligibility Requirements

As illustrated in Exhibit 3.1, a resource inventory should include eligibility requirements. Services may apparently be available to a population but may not be accessible to all. A nationwide inventory of mental health resources (Longest, Konan, & Tweed, 1979) classified services as follows:

available	if offered in the catchment area (a region served by a community mental health center);
accessible	if available without eligibility requirements; and
comprehensive	if all four target services were accessible

Only 29% of the 1499 catchment areas in the nation were found to have comprehensive mental health services.

Target population characteristics can be compared with eligibility requirements to identify gaps in services. Characteristics of the target population that are examined should be mutually exclusive and locally meaningful, and should correspond to relevant federal and state aid requirements. Typical categories are age, sex, and race.

3.6 Service Capacity

A resource inventory becomes more useful for need analyses when, besides information on *who* provides *what* services, information is included on *how much* of a service is or can be offered. Differences between agencies and practitioners on how service utilization is recorded can make measuring capacity difficult. Table 3.4 presents four measures of service utilization and problems that can arise with each.

As part of the information gathered for the resource inventory, agencies should be queried about the level of services provided to the various target population groups, including both demographics and place of residence. What measure, or combination of measures, of capacity is best depends on the services being inventoried. Sometimes, as in education, there is a commonly accepted measure such as full time equivalent (FTE) student or instructor. Even with full coverage of

TABLE 3.4
Approaches to Measuring Service Utilization

Number of persons	Many clients use a service more than once. Unduplicated counts are preferred. Definition of such terms as "resident" varies from program to program.
Number of events	Admissions or terminations are often used. Admissions generally indicate new clients although it may reflect a formal process that is not always followed. Terminations may be due to nonuse of service for a period of time.
Units of service	Events are not the same as service. Actual services provided in one unit, for example, patient day, may vary greatly from agency to agency.
Staff time	This is the greatest determinant of cost for human services and education; who is a staff member and percentage time assigned to task vary; support requirements differ between units.
Cost of program	Client mix, unionization, and accreditation all will contribute to differences in cost between agencies.

service providers and an adequate measure, service capacity estimates can be inaccurate because of slippage (use of services from outside areas by the target population) and seepage (use of the area's services by those from outside the area).

Estimates of service utilization (the number of clients being served) or service capacity (the number of clients who could be served) can be combined with estimates of how many people could or should use the service (see Chapters 4 and 5) to determine whether there is a need for additional services or expanded capacity. Exhibit 3.2 gives an example of this use of resource inventory.

Exhibit 3.2
Hypertension Service Needs

Petersen, Bosanac, Baranowski, and Forren (1981) developed a resource inventory as part of a need analysis for hypertension programming in the state of West Virginia. Four types of service providers (physicians, pharmacists, health agencies, and voluntary agencies) were surveyed in each of the state's eleven planning and development regions. This included four types of hypertension services: prevention, screening, medical care, and patient education. Five mailings plus telephone follow-ups were used to get a 90% completion rate.

Providers were asked about the types of services they provided, how frequently they were offered, the number of people served, and the number of additional people they could serve. Besides resource inventory information, the number of hypertensives in each of the eleven subregions was estimated from national statistics on the prevalence of hypertension. National hypertension rates by age, sex, and race were combined with the population profiles of each subregion to develop the estimates by synthetic estimation (Section 4.2).

Three indices of need were computed for each subregion for each of the four types of service:

Density	the ratio of the estimated number of hypertensives to the number of providers indicating they offer the service. This is a measure of the availability of service; the lower the ratio the more available the service.
Intensity	the ratio of the estimated number of hypertensives to the units of service (number of events). This is a measure of the availability of services; the lower the ratio the more available the service.
Participation	the ratio of the number of providers indicating they offer the service to the total number of providers. This is a measure of unused capacity; the lower the ratio the greater the unused capacity.

Problems within a subregion would be indicated if density and intensity ratios were high, indicating that there were many hypertensives for each service provider or unit of service. A potential solution to problems of unavailable services is indicated if the participation ratio were low. Providers currently in the subregion might be induced to begin offering services. Comparative expectations were used to determine if the indices were high or low. Each of the subregions was ranked on each indices from the best (1) to the worst (11).

Table 3.5 presents a profile of capacity indicators for two services in one subregion. The second column of the table presents the rank of the subregion compared to others in the state. For screenings, intensity is much lower than density. This pattern indicates that the service is provided by relatively few of the potential providers surveyed. The participation ratio indicates that there is a capacity to expand this service.

Medical care shows the same pattern of intensity/density ranks as screening. Participation, although ranked low, is high overall and does not differ much between subregions. Note the intensity score for medical

TABLE 3.5
Capacity Indices for Two Hypertension Services,
for One of Eleven Subregions

Capacity Index	Screenings Score	Rank	Medical Care Score	Rank
Density	212.88	7	323.30	7
Intensity	25.59	3	.67	4
Participation	.51	9	.70	9

care, an event measure, is less than one. This indicates more events than estimated hypertensives. Not every person with hypertension is receiving medical care! Rather, those receiving care experience multiple events. Unduplicated counts of people served would have yielded a more accurate intensity ratio.

The rankings on intensity for both these services probably indicate little need in this subregion for additional services. Subregions with higher intensity ranks should need greater attention.

3.7 Strengths and Weaknesses

A resource inventory is a solution-oriented component of a need analysis. First, resource inventories describe the services available to a target population. Second, resource inventories can reveal gaps in services, due to lack of availability, lack of accessibility, lack of continuity, or lack of capacity. Gaps can point out groups or regions where individuals are at risk. Depending on the problems of the target population, gaps may indicate a need for additional programming. Third, a resource inventory may point to underutilized services, where additional services may be available at a small cost. Finally, resource inventories help agencies and funding bodies avoid launching services and programs where there is already a good deal of competition.

By itself a resource inventory does not indicate need. Just because solutions are not available, does not mean they are needed. Measures of the extent of problems and potential demand are required. Solutions suggested by a resource inventory are those already being implemented. Resource inventories may give a status quo, service-agency orientation to solutions.

EXERCISES

1. Consider a service you have used in the last month. How many alternatives for this service were available? Using resources available to you (e.g., yellow pages and colleagues), develop a resource inventory for this service in your town.

2. Develop a measure of service utilization for some program of interest. Contact two providers of this service and discuss the strengths and weaknesses of this measure.

3. What drawbacks are there to the use of gaps discovered through resource inventories to indicate need? (Hint: consider which of Bradshaw's (1972) outcome expectations are fulfilled by a resource inventory.)

4

Social Indicator Analyses

Social indicators are aggregate statistical measures that depict important aspects of a social situation and of underlying historical trends and developments. Through synthetic estimation, characteristics of subgroups can be estimated from data about a larger group. Risk factors are social indicators that predict undesirable outcomes such as admission to a mental hospital. Risk factors can be indicators of need for services. Census and other national indicators, including the Mental Health Demographic Profile System, are discussed. The comparison of client profiles with target population descriptions is presented as part of need analysis.

A primary question in need analysis is who (the target population or market) is potentially in need of services. This descriptive information has many uses: (a) it sets a boundary on the potential problems and solutions; (b) it reveals characteristics of the population that can be related to problems and service usage; and (c) when combined with information on use of services, it shows utilization patterns for subgroups. Often the chief source of information on target populations is descriptive statistics found in public records and reports, such as the decennial census of population and housing conducted by the U.S. Department of Commerce (Kaplan & Van Valey, 1980).

4.1 What Is a Social Indicator?

Social indicators are aggregate statistical measures that depict important aspects of a social situation and of underlying historical trends and developments. They usually are not gathered for the need analysis itself but are local, state, or federal government statistics. Social indicators usually are available only for large groups of people and are tied to a specific geographical area. Social indicator information is inexpensive to gather and allows useful normative comparisons.

Social indicators take many forms. First, they describe populations, for example, ethnicity, age, or place of residence. Second, they describe government expenditures and other inputs, for example, spending on

education or number of physicians. Third, they measure social welfare
or quality of life, for example, crime rates and unemployment. Social
indicators are often considered "objective" or "hard data." Finally, they
reveal *problems* rather than *solutions* in a need analysis. Besides
measuring problems directly, indicators may point to those at risk of
developing problems.

The most important source of social indicators is the government:
federal, state, and local. The federal government publishes a tre-
mendous amount of quantitative information derived from various
censuses and surveys (see Section 4.4). Much of this information is
deposited in the 1200+ Federal Depository Libraries[1] (Federal Depository Library Program, 1983). The best single index to the federal
information is the *American Statistical Index*, a comprehensive guide to
the statistical publications of the U.S. Government. Other useful indices
are the *CIS Annual Index* to Congressional publications and public
laws and the *Monthly Catalog of U.S. Government Publications*.

4.2 Target Population Description

Identifying relevant characteristics of target populations begins with
service eligibility requirements and agency mission statements. Colleges
have education and age restrictions for their student bodies. Human
service agencies have income, disability, and geographic restrictions for
their clients. Agency mission statements may limit services by sex, or by
religious and ethnic group membership. Target population descriptions
should identify the number of potential clients within each of the
eligibility and mission restrictions. For example, if an agency is
targeting senior women with income of less than $5,000 a year, it is the
population with this combination of characteristics that needs to be
described.

Beyond eligibility restrictions, target population descriptions should
include important demographic characteristics:

- age
- income
- sex
- ethnicity
- location of population

A more detailed analysis may be required to identify specific problems and solutions.

Synthetic Estimation

Sometimes, a critical eligibility criterion is not available for the target population but is for some larger population, for example, the nation. Small area estimates of a characteristic can be obtained from data for larger areas by synthetic estimation (Holzer, Jackson, & Tweed, 1981). This procedure assumes that prevalence[2] rates for demographic groups from smaller areas are the same as rates for these demographic groups on a larger level. If national statistics reveal that 34% of the men and 49% of the women over 65 have hypertension, the same proportion of senior men and women would be expected to have hypertension on the state or county level. Differences in the prevalence of hypertension from the smaller (e.g., county) to larger (e.g., national) level are assumed to be due to differences in the distribution of demographic characteristics and not in susceptibility to hypertension. Exhibit 3.2 used synthetic estimation to determine the need for hypertension services. Exhibit 4.1 presents a detailed example of synthetic estimation for estimating the need for birth control and pregnancy counseling.

Exhibit 4.1
Estimating the Frequencies of Births
and of Abortions of a College Campus

The Student Health Service at a large midwestern state university wanted to estimate the number of births and abortions among its student body. These numbers were used in planning pregnancy and birth control counseling. Analysis of university records revealed an average daily female student population of 5659, 90% single, and 85% between 18 and 25 years of age. The information from national birth rates and abortion ratios (shown in Table 4.1) was used to estimate the frequencies of pregnancies and abortions for the student body for a 12-month period. (Techniques for computing rates and ratios are presented in Section 5.1.) For example, for every 1000 single female college students between 18 and 25, national statistics predict 40 births and 55 abortions during a year. Births are predicted by multiplying the

TABLE 4.1
Birth Rate and Abortion Ratio by
Age and Marital Status of Mother, 1980

	Birth Rate[a]		Abortion Ratio[b]	
Age	Married	Single	Married	Single
15-17	407.2	20.6	50.7[c]	1119.8[c]
18-24	217.4	40.2	74.3	1376.3
25-49	58.2	29.9	88.1	1600.3

NOTE: Race of mother was not included because the racial distribution of the student body approximated that of the nation. The female student body was 9% black.
a. Number of live births per 1000 women. Adapted from the National Center for Health Statistics *Advanced Report of Final Natality Statistics, 1980.*
b. Number of abortions per 1000 live births. Adapted from abortion reporting data for 11 states for 1979 made available by the National Center for Health Statistics.
c. Abortion ratios are for the 10-17 age group.

birth rate for the subgroup population by the number in the group. This product is then divided by the base for the birth rate (1000). Abortions are estimated by multiplying the number of (expected) births by the abortion ratios for the group. The product is then divided by the base for the abortion ratio (1000).

Table 4.2 illustrates how a target population description (column 1) and national statistics (columns 2 and 4) are combined in synthetic estimation. For example, the number of births expected for the single students between 18 and 24 is computed by multiplying the number in the population (4585 in column 1) by the birth rate for this group (40.2 in column 2) and dividing the product by 1000 (the base for the birth rate). On the basis of national statistics, this group of students was expected to have 184 births. The number of abortions for this group is estimated by multiplying the number of births (184 in column 3) by the abortion ratio (1376.3 in column 4), and dividing the product by 1000. A total of 252 abortions was expected. For the entire student body, national statistics predict 270 births and 280 abortions during one year. Other factors, such as the social class of the students or the effectiveness of programming at the university, may affect the accuracy of this prediction.

Social Area Analysis

Social area analysis (Holzer & Robbins, 1981; Piasecki & Kamis-Gould, 1981) provides another framework for describing urban target

TABLE 4.2
Synthetic Estimation of Number of Births and Abortions
to the Student Body for One Year

Age	Marital Status	Number in Population	Birth-rate[a]	Expected Number of Births (1) x (2)/1000	Abortion Ratio[a]	Expected Number of Births (3) x (4)/1000
15-17	Married	2	407.2	1	50.7	0
	Single	94	20.6	2	1119.8	2
18-24	Married	233	217.4	51	74.3	4
	Single	4585	40.2	184	1376.3	253
25+	Married	347	58.2	20	88.1	2
	Single	398	29.9	12	1600.3	19
Totals		5659		270		280

a. From Table 4.1.

populations. A substantial body of research supports description of the population of a geographical area by three classes of indicators:

Social rank   a general index of social status including occupational status and education;

Family status   family composition, type of residence, and women's labor force participation; and

Ethnicity   proportion of population black or other minority

These indicators reveal reliable and meaningful differences between urban areas. In addition, areas of low social rank, with large proportions of nonfamily households and that have large minority populations have been found to be in need of a wide range of human services. Goldsmith, Ungler, Windle, Shambaugh, and Rosen (1981) have produced an excellent self-teaching manual on social area analysis built on the Mental Health Demographic Profile System (MHDPS) described in Section 4.4.

4.3 Risk Factor Analysis

By far the most frequent use of social indicators is risk factor analysis. Social indicators are chosen on the basis of their ability to predict problems or use of services at the individual level. For example, epidemiologic surveys have found that an individual's social status reliably predicts survey measures of mental dysfunction. Also, studies find that admissions to mental hospitals and use of out-patient facilities can be predicted by client characteristics. Such individual level findings are used to select and justify group indicators of potential need. For example, the relationship between social rank and depression in an epidemiologic survey leads to the inference that counties with higher proportions of population in low status jobs have greater need of mental health services for depression.

Generalization from individual to aggregate level findings (and back again) has been labeled an *ecological fallacy*, because it is often not justified logically or empirically. For example, Milcarek and Link (1981) found that ethnicity indicators, but not those related to marital status, survived individual to group level generalization as predictors of use of mental health service at the census tract level in New York City. Ethnicity was related to use of mental health resources both at the individual and the group levels. Marital status was related to use of mental health resources only at the individual level. Areas with high divorced or single populations did not use more mental health resources, although both admissions and outpatient visits predicted this pattern. Considerable work is currently under way to validate the use of social indicators as predictors of mental health problems (Ciarlo & Shern, 1985; Regier et al., 1984).

Working with Risk Indicators

Social indicator analyses can compare regions or subregions within the area served by an agency on multiple measures of risk. Direct comparison between different social indicators is difficult because the measures often are not in the same metric and because distributions are not similar. When multiple indicators are used, a method for combining results is necessary. Many solutions are available (see Section 9.1):

1. *Standardization.* This technique treats indicators as if they are interval measures. Observed scores are transformed to *z* scores by this formula:

$$z = \frac{\text{Observed score for subregion} \quad - \quad \text{Average score for all subregions}}{\text{standard deviation of all observed scores}}$$

Z score transformation allow social indicators to be added across (all or meaningful subgroups) for an index of need (Cagle, 1984). Some interpret z scores > 1.0 as an indicator of need for services (e.g., Warheit & Bell, 1983).

2. *Percentile Ratings.* This technique treats indicators as ordinal measures. Subregions are ranked on an indicator and this ranking is converted into percentiles. Alternately (as in the MHDPS described in Section 4.4) percentiles can be computed on a national level for similar subregions. Percentile can be interpreted according to these rules (Goldsmith et al., 1981):

- <10th........ Extremely low
- 10th-30th....Low
- 30th-50th....Low Moderate
- 50th-70th....High Moderate
- 70th-90th....High
- 90th+........ Extremely High

3. *Ranking,* either directly from observed scores, or after transformation to z scores and percentiles. Subregions are ranked on each social indicator and assigned a score based on their rank order. These ranks are then added to give an overall ranking of subregions. Table 4.3 gives an example. Counties are ranked from the greatest to the least (5) needy. County A is ranked as most needy on indicators X and Z and ranked number 4 on indicator Y. County A is the most needy county because the sum of its ranks (6) is lower than the sum of ranks for any of the other counties.

4. *Prevalence of risk.* The number of people at risk in each subregion is computed for each indicator (e.g., the number of persons in poverty, the number of teenagers not in school). These numbers are then added. Need is indicated by the total number of people at risk in the subregion.

The appropriateness of any of these methods of transforming social indicators depends on the constraints of the particular need analysis. Often justification is sought through multivariate statistics. Integration of multiple sources of information is discussed in detail in Chapter 9.

The results of risk indicator analysis are often displayed on a map. Seriousness of problems revealed for each subregion is indicated by the color, usually the darkness of the shading, of the region on the map.

TABLE 4.3
Example of Combining Multiple Social Indicators by Ranking

| | Rank of Social Indicator | | | |
County	X	Y	Z	Overall Rank
A	1	4	1	1
B	2	1	4	2
C	3	3	2	3
D	4	5	3	5
E	5	2	3	4

Although, as discussed in Section 10.3, maps can create false impressions, they can communicate a great deal of information in a form familiar to lay audiences.

Market Segmentation

The designation "risk factor analysis" implies that the only target population characteristics worth analyzing are predictors of problems. This is not the case. Indicators of strengths (e.g., education, cultural, and regional assets) may be appropriate and useful. The marketing model discussed in Chapter 2 suggests segmentation of the target population into distinct and meaningful groups of users for purposes of analysis and planning. Dimensions of segmentation are often suggested as a result of client or community surveys (Sections 6.5 and 6.7) or the observation of current service use patterns (Chapter 5). Segmentation may be on demographics, geographic areas, lifestyle (Bernstein, 1978), or income—whatever characteristics are associated with differential use or potential use of services. Often the segments that offer the most attractive market are identified and studied in depth.

4.4 National Indicators

The federal government collects and publishes a wide range of census and survey statistics on health, births, deaths, crime, education, and other topics. Much of this information is available for demographic subgroups and for geographical subregions, particularly states. Units of state and local governments also collect economic and social indicators,

TABLE 4.4
Summary Descriptions of Population Questions
in the 1980 U.S. Census

100% Sample	17% Sample
Name	Current language
Household relationship	Ancestry
Sex	Place of residence 5 years ago and major
Race	activity 5 years ago
Age	Age screener
Marital status	Veteran status
Spanish/Hispanic origin or descent	Presence of disability or limiting work or use
Coverage questions	of public transportation
	Children ever born
17% Sample	Date of first marriage and whether
	terminated by death
School enrollment	Employment and unemployment
Educational attainment	Place of work and journey to work
Place of birth	Industry, occupation and class of worker
Citizenship and year of immigration	Work and weeks looking for work in 1979
	Sources of income and total income in 1979

as well as maintaining nationally collected indicators for local and regional areas.

U.S. Census

Every ten years the U.S. Department of Commerce conducts a census of population and housing. This information is organized by geographic and political units and allows both historical and interarea comparisons. Geographic and political units vary from the nation as a whole to city blocks in urban areas, averaging 100 residents, and enumerated districts elsewhere, averaging about 800 residents (Kaplan & Van Valey, 1980). Printed compilations of census statistics are available for larger political areas (e.g., county and state) though smaller units may require special analyses.[3] Some of the more useful geographical areas are as follows:

SMSA   Standard Metropolitan Statistical Area. Metropolitan county or counties that are economically related and include a city with at least 50,000 residents.

| census tracts | statistical but locally meaningful subdivision of metropolitan counties with an average of 4,000 residents. Census tracts can be aggregated to equal the county. |
| MCD | Minor Civil Division, legal subdivisions of counties that are not or are only partially divided into census tracts. Minor civil divisions and census tracts, where they exist, can be aggregated to equal the county. |

Table 4.4 summarizes questions from the 1980 census of population, those asked of everyone and those asked only of a sample. Some of these items have been combined to create derived variables (e.g., poverty status in 1979). The Mental Health Demographic Profile System (MHDPS), discussed in the next section, provides an example of the richness of the analyses possible using the census information.

Despite its availability and easy comparability, census information should be analyzed for validity, for reliability, and for timeliness. Problems with use of group level data in risk factor analysis have been mentioned: (a) Ecological fallacies threaten generalizations from group to individual level findings, and vice versa; (b) the validity of group level relationships, for example, between social indicators and admissions to mental hospitals, has not been well established; and (c) social indicators are, at best, predictors of problems, not solutions.

Census data are often regarded as objective, or "hard," data. This judgment is not justified. In the 1960 census, 0% of the forms were self-administered. In the 1970 census, 60% of the forms were self-administered. In the 1980 census, 90% of the forms were self-administered! The U.S. census has become a mailed survey. Racial status provides an example. The 1980 census saw a 60% increase in those of "Spanish/Hispanic" origin. In the 1960 and 1970 censuses, almost all the Spanish population were recorded or recorded themselves as racially "white" or "black." In the 1980 census 40% of this population indicated their race was "other." Like all mailed surveys, the census depends on the understanding and the care taken by respondents in answering questions.

Probably the largest drawback to using census data is its timeliness. The census is not valid for areas undergoing rapid change. After a 10-year period, the accuracy of the census can be challenged for many parts of the country.

Mental Health Demographic Profile System
MHDPS

The Mental Health Demographic Profile System (MHDPS) was developed from the 1970 census by NIMH to assist community mental health centers plan and evaluate their service programs (Rosen & Goldsmith, 1981). Census data were selected to characterize the community on social area analysis dimensions and to identify high risk populations. The 130+ indicators were available by community mental health center catchment area, as well as other census divisions. The 1980 version, renamed the Health Demographic Profile System (HDPS) (Goldsmith, Jackson, Doenhoefer, Johnson, Tweed, Barbano, & Warheit, 1984), has recently been released to the states, typically the department of mental health, and will soon be available from the National Technical Information Service.[4] The new version has been enhanced, and includes both direct and derived indicators specially chosen for relevance to human service planning. HDPS indicators are available by state, county, census tract, and minor civil division. The latter two can be aggregated to cover most geographical areas. Working with the system should be considerably easier than working with raw census information.

The system includes the following seven categories of social indicators:

(1) general population data, including rural/urban distinctions
(2) ethnic composition
(3) indicators of social rank, including economic and social status
(4) indicators of family structure, including age distributions and marital status
(5) housing characteristics, including type, condition and crowding
(6) indicators of community stability, including residential mobility and migration
(7) disabled population

Each category includes indicators of high risk for physical and mental disorders as well as indicators related to children, to women, and to older persons.

4.5 Client Analysis

The discrepancy model provides a powerful use of target population descriptions. Comparisons between population estimates (what ought to be) and profiles of the current client/customer population (what is) can reveal gaps in services (Bachrach & Zautra, 1980). Analysis of client records (described in more detail in Chapter 5) yield many of the same demographic variables used in social indicator analysis, as well as information on services used and diagnoses. Comparison is made between the proportion of any particular subgroup in the target population and the proportion of this subgroup in the client population. Heavy and light service users (e.g., competitive and untapped market segments) can be identified.

In conducting client analysis, expectations are developed for the number of subgroup members that should use services. The following are four common assumptions:

(1) The same proportion of all groups should use services, for example, 2%. If less than 2% of a subgroup has used services, underuse may indicate need.

(2) Subgroups should use services in direct proportion to their frequency in the target population. If those 65 and over represent 15% of the target population, they should represent 15% of the client population.

(3) Subgroups should use services in proportion to their presence in an at-risk population. If males make up 75% of those at risk for alcoholism, they should make up a similar percentage of clients in an alcohol counseling program.

(4) The subgroup or subregion having the highest proportion served is used as a standard, for example, the school district with the highest immunization rate. The performance of other groups or regions is evaluated against this proportion of service.

Exhibit 4.2 presents an example of client analysis.

Exhibit 4.2
Client Analysis at a
Community Mental Health Center

Column 1 of Table 4.5 presents the 1980 target population description by sex and by age for the population served by a community mental health center in a largely rural midwestern county. The source is the

1980 U.S. census. Column 2 presents the profile of these demographic categories from the client records. The indicator here is unduplicated admissions; thus no person was counted more than once. Overall 1.5% of the county's population was served by the community mental health center during the 1983-1984 fiscal year. Assuming that subgroups, here determined by sex and age, should be served in proportion to their presence in the population leads to the expectation that 1.5% of each group would be admitted to the center. This expectation is shown in column 3 of the table.

Column 4 compares the expectation with the actual admissions. Expectations closely parallel admissions for sex. Nine more men were admitted than expected and nine fewer women were admitted than expected. Expectations were not met for the age groupings. Adults (25-44) were the only group not admitted less than expected. The 25-44 age group showed 2 times the number of admissions expected! The most underserved group was young adults (15-24). The inference of need requires information on other services available to the group (Chapter 3) and on use analysis (Chapter 5).

4.6 Strengths and Weaknesses

Strengths and weaknesses of social indicators have been reviewed in the section above on national indicators (Section 4.4). On the positive side, social indicators are available on most topics and geographical areas, and are inexpensive and simple to use. Social indicators are especially useful for describing populations, both absolutely and comparatively. Social indicators can be used as proxy measures of problems. Because social indicators often reflect quantities rather than judgments, they are not perceived as possessing a bias and have credibility as "hard data."

On the negative side, social indicators have questionable validity as predictors of problems, both the empirical association with criterion measures and the generalization across levels of analysis. Social indicators may reveal problems, but do not show solutions. Whether identified areas are in need depends on the services currently available (Chapter 3) and on the cost and effectiveness of additional programming. Social indicator analyses are better for larger rather than smaller areas. Relationships demonstrated on the state or national level may not generalize to more homogeneous subregions.

TABLE 4.5
Client Analysis for Rural County
Community Mental Health Center

	(1) 1980 Target Population	(2) Unduplicated 1983-84 Admissions	(3) Expected Admissions (1)* .01525[a]	(4) Over or (Under) Admissions (2)−(3)
Men	31905	495	486	9
Women	29617	443	452	(9)
0-14	10089	79	154	(75)
15-24	21704	229	331	(102)
25-44	15234	473	232	241
45-64	8485	122	129	(7)
65+	6010	35	92	(57)
Total	61522	938	938	

a. During the 1983-84 fiscal year admissions made up this proportion of the county's population, that is, 936/61522.

TABLE 4.6
Percentage of the U.S. Adult Population 20% or
More Overweight, 1971-1974, by Age and Sex

	Percentage of Group 20% or More Overweight	
Age	Men	Women
20-24	7.4	9.6
25-34	13.6	17.1
35-44	17.0	24.3
45-54	15.8	27.8
55-64	15.1	34.7
65-74	13.4	31.5

SOURCE: Adapted from Abraham and Johnson (1979)

EXERCISES

1. Select an indicator of social rank (e.g., median family income) and family structure (e.g., ratio of those 65 and over to those 25-64). Examine the changes in the place of your early childhood (city, town, county) on these variables as well as the age-sex distribution over the 1960, the 1970, and the 1980 censuses. Use the age categories (0-17, 18-24, 25-44, 45-64, and 65 and over).

2. Estimate the proportion of the population of your city or county who are overweight using synthetic estimation and the information in Table 4.6. How has the prevalence of this condition changed over the last 20 years?

TABLE 4.7
Data for Client Analysis, Exercise 3

Class Standing	Number in Student Body	Number Counseled During Year	Not Using Birth Control When Sexually Active[a]
Freshman	1898	19	34%
Sophomore	1695	28	38%
Junior	1496	40	25%
Senior	1825	42	18%
Graduate	1073	15	14%

a. An at-risk indicator resulting from a survey of the student body.

3. Do a client analysis for a college birth control counseling program with a target population and client profile as shown in Table 4.7: (a) assume services should be rendered in proportion to presence in student body; (b) assume services should be rendered in proportion to presence in at-risk population. Compare the results of these assumptions.

NOTES

1. Libraries are, of course, an excellent source of ideas and information at all stages in need analysis. Literature is probably available on the problems of most target populations (at some level of abstraction) and on solutions that have been tried with the population.

2. Prevalence is the number of people in a population who have a condition. Incidence is the number of people who develop the condition during a particular time period. Both quantities are often expressed by rates or proportions of the total population.

3. For information and assistance in analyzing census data contact the Data Users Service Division, Bureau of the Census, Washington, D.C. 20233, (301) 763-2400.

4. National Technical Information Service, U. S. Department of Commerce, 5285 Port Royal Rd., Springfield, Virginia, 22161, (703) 487-4807.

5

Analyzing Use of Services

Use of services is crucial to programming in the human services and education. Utilization experiences of other agencies, epidemiological estimates of the incidence of problems, and professional standards are sources of expectations for use of a program agency or service. Rate and ratio formulas are explained. Use analysis combines expected use with analysis of actual clients seen and services provided by an agency or program. Use analysis includes examination of potential barriers: awareness, availability, accessibility, and acceptability. Alternative interpretations indicate that heavy use is an indicator of need, that light use is an indicator of need, and that use is not directly related to need.

Examining *solutions* to problems involves estimating how much use will be made of the solutions. Development of a service or program that will be *used* is important to all need analysis models. Few agencies or governmental units can afford to fund services that are not used. Use analysis is based on comparative expectations: Patterns of utilization for one group indicate patterns for another. Use can be predicted from the experience of current programs or programs offered to a similar population. Use can be compared among subgroups of the target population. This chapter discusses analysis and extrapolation from utilization information.

First, rates and ratios are introduced and their use in prediction is discussed. The choice of rates based on professional standards is presented. Then, finally, steps in use analysis are described.

5.1 Computing Rates, Ratios, and Other Indices

Rates of admissions, of services provided, or of people trained in a certain period of time, are basic to use analysis. A rate is a fraction, with a numerator (the top) and a denominator (the bottom). The numerator comes from agency records and the denominator from the target population description (Section 4.2). The numerator is the number of people served or number of services provided; the denominator is the number *eligible* in the population. Because numerators are based on agency records they are usually easier to compute than denominators.

For ease of presentation and understanding, the denominator of a rate is a multiple of 100, called the base. We are familiar with the base of 100, a percentage—7% is an incidence of 7 occurrences in 100 opportunities. The base used is arbitrary, but important to communication and understanding. Bases of 1000 and 100,000 are common. For example, a community college attracts students at a rate of 150 per 1000 high school graduates in its service area. This rate is equivalent to and easier to think about than 117/781, which might be the actual rate. Similarly, it is easier to visualize an increase from 700 per 100,000 to 1400 per 100,000 than from .7% to 1.4%.

Rates apply in many areas. The incidence of a disease is the rate of new cases (numerator) divided by the population at risk (denominator) and multiplied by some base. An admission rate is the number of people admitted to a program divided by the number eligible for the program and multiplied by some base. If use rates are computed separately for subregions of a service area, we might call it a "penetration index," measuring the depth of services provided to eligibles in each subregion.

Table 5.1 presents rates and ratios common in use analyses. The first, a use rate, divides the number of individuals served by the number eligible and then multiplies this fraction by the base (e.g., 1000). For the community college example above where 117 students enrolled out of 781 high school graduates:

use rate (per 1000) = (117/781) $\times$ 1000 = 150.

The participation ratio of Exhibit 3.2 could be turned into a rate by multiplying by a base, for example, 1000. The screening participation ratio of .51, from Table 3.5, is equivalent to a rate of 510 per 1000.

A use ratio, the second entry in Table 5.1, compares two services (e.g., abortions to births in Exhibit 4.1), characteristics of two populations (e.g., hourly pay of women to hourly pay of men), or some measure of services to number of people served (e.g., faculty to student ratios). The intensity and density ratios of Exhibit 3.2 are examples of use ratios.

The third formula in Table 5.1 is an index of the fit between use and expectations. If it is positive, use exceeds expectations, if it is negative use falls short of expectations. It occurs frequently in client analyses (Section 4.5). Some authors refer to it as the percentage of *unmet need*. For an example, examine the final column of Table 5.3.

TABLE 5.1
Rates, Ratios, and Other Formulas
of Analyzing Utilization of Services

Use rate	$\dfrac{\text{Number of people served}}{\text{Number of eligibles}} \times \text{Base}$
Use ratio	$\dfrac{\text{Rate or number for Group 1}}{\text{Rate or number for Group 2}}$
Percentage underserved	$\dfrac{\text{Number of people served} - \text{number expected}}{\text{Number expected}} \times 100$

5.2 Predicting Use

Utilization experience of other agencies, epidemiological estimates of the incidence of problems, and professional standards are sources of expectations for use of a program agency or service. Comparing expectations to actual use reveals discrepancies (problems). As an example, Table 5.2 presents national admission rates for mental health and psychiatric services during 1975 (Rosenstein & Milazzo-Sayre, 1981). For the entire nation, there were 1690 mental health admissions for every 100,000 people. This rate provides a comparative expectation (Section 1.2) for use of a particular agency. After examining barriers to use (Section 5.4), underuse may be interpreted as a need for additional services, as a need for improved service delivery, or as an expression of a lack of need for services.

Longest et al. (1979) developed expectations for community mental health services from the distribution of services currently available in the nation's 1499 catchment areas. Capacity was measured by the rate of unrestricted services available per 1000 population. Services were judged adequate if capacity was greater than that found in 20% of all catchment areas. If capacity was lower than that in 20% of the catchment areas, services were judged inadequate. Inpatient mental health services were adequate if there were more than thirteen beds per 10,000 catchment area residents. Day care services were adequate if there were more than 1.5 hours of care available per 1000 catchment area population. Outpatient services were adequate if the staff treatment hours available per 1000 population were greater than 3.01.

TABLE 5.2
Admission Rates per 100,000 for Mental Health Facilities
By Age and Sex, United States, 1975

Age	Total	Male	Female	Male/Female Ratio
All ages	1690	1768	1618	1.1
0-17	989	1169	801	1.5
18-24	2299	2433	2173	1.1
25-44	2727	2589	2856	0.9
45-64	1597	1748	1459	1.2
65+	785	793	780	1.0

SOURCE: Adapted from Rosenstein & Milazzo-Sayre, 1981.

When comparisons of use rates are made between agencies or programs, rates may need to be adjusted for differences in population characteristics. Adjustments should be made for characteristics that are important predictors of the rate. For example, pregnancy is strongly related to age and marital status. Before the pregnancy rate for a college campus can be compared to that of the nation, national rates should be adjusted for age and marital status (Exhibit 4.1). Frequent adjustments are for age and sex. Rates are computed separately for age and sex categories and then projected on some standard age-sex population distribution. If one program serves a population that is 60% male and 40% female and another serves a program that is 70% female and 30% male, an overall use rate for each might be computed as if they served a population that was 50% male and 50% female. The choice of appropriate national or state norms and of adjustments depends on the program being studied and on the normative statistics available. On the basis of survey responses, Veroff, Kukla, and Dourvan (1981) report that women use social services more than men, the younger use more services than the older, and that the educated use more services than the uneducated.

Exhibit 5.1 applies national use rates to help interpret a local agency's utilization experience.

Exhibit 5.1
Use Analysis for A
Community Mental Health Center

Exhibit 5.1 is based on the same data as Exhibit 4.2: unduplicated admissions at a community mental health center servicing a largely rural midwestern county. The target population description and actual admissions are presented in Table 4.4. Table 5.3 shows utilization rates for the center, by sex and age, and rates from federally funded community mental health centers. These latter rates provide comparative expectations for use.

Except for the 15-24 year-old age group, the community mental health center had higher utilization rates than did the federally funded centers. Overall the rural center had 47% more admissions than would be expected from the federally funded centers. Compared to other subgroups served by this center (as discussed in Exhibit 4.2) and to national experience, the 15-24 year old age group is underserved. This pattern may reflect need for services, competition (the presence of a university with its own counseling center), or effective prevention activities.

Epidemiological Estimates

Expectations for use have been developed from epidemiologic surveys that identify the "true prevalence" of problems. For example, after reviewing epidemiologic research, Link and Dohrenwend (1980) conclude that between 16% and 25% of Americans have serious mental problems, although no more than 25% of these ever receive treatment. Certain demographic groups consistently have been found to score higher than others on survey tests of mental impairment (Dohrenwend et al., 1980; Link & Dohrenwend, 1980). A higher-than-average presence of such groups in a target population leads to expectations of greater need for services. Discrepancies between expectations and actual use rates for such groups indicate problems. In recognition of this relationship, allocation formulas often link the size of the population with, or at-risk for, a problem and the need for services. The number of people with a problem is computed for each area and funds are distributed in proportion to this number.

Exhibit 5.2 examines the relationship between the size of the at-risk or problem population and the use of services. Problems are indicated where there is a discrepancy between these measures.

Exhibit 5.2
Indicator-Risk Predictions of Utilization

Lobb, Young, and Ciarlo (1979) developed expectations for use of mental health services based on social indicators. Expectations were

TABLE 5.3
Use Analysis for Rural County
Community Mental Health Center,
See Table 4.4 for Columns 1 and 2

	(3) Utilization Rate per 1000 (2)/(1)* 1000	(4) 1974 Federal CMHC Utilization Rates per 1000	(5) Expected Admissions (4)*(1)/1000	(6) Percentage Over or Under (−) (2)−(5)/(5)
Men	15.5	10.3	328	51
Women	15.0	10.5	312	42
0-14	7.8	6.2	63	26
15-24	10.6	15.3	332	−31
25-44	31.0	16.4	250	89
45-64	14.4	8.2	70	74
65+	5.8	3.9	24	48
Total	15.2	10.4	640	47

NOTE: Source for federal utilization rates is Rosenstein & Bass (1979).

compared to mental health service use rates for census tracts in Denver. Multiple social indicators were identified to tap three factors found to be related to need for mental health services: population size, social ratio of divorced disorganization (e.g., number of divorces and separated males per 1000 married males), and social affluence (e.g., median value of owner-occupied housing units). Large population size, presence of social disorganization, and lack of social affluence indicated need for services. Each census tract was given a score (similar to a z-score, Section 4.3) on each factor. These scores were averaged to form a standardized measure of need for services. It was assumed that, if the needs of all census tracts were being met equally, the number of clients served from the tract would be predicted from the standardized measure of need.

The place of residence of all clients admitted during the year was coded for the six public mental health agencies and for the state hospital serving the Denver area. Analyses identified the number of clients served for each census tract. Overall 15,000 clients were served, averaging 123 per census tract with a standard deviation of 108.5. Expected number of clients served for each census tract was computed using this formula:

$$\text{expected number of clients} = (\text{need} * 108.5) + 123$$

where need was the average score on the three social indicator factors. The expected number of clients served was then compared to the actual number of clients served in each census tract. Discrepancies were used as an input for allocation of new resources.

Cautions for Predicting Use

Where comparative and normative estimates of use are available, they must be interpreted cautiously. In a classic paper, Wennberg & Gittelsohn (1973) found wide variation in use of health care among small regions in Vermont, with the greatest utilization concentrated in areas of greatest wealth. Appendectomies varied from 10 to 32 per 10,000 and surgery on varicose veins varied from 6 to 28 per 10,000. Regier, Goldberg, Kessler, & Burns (1980) found similar diversity in use of outpatient mental health services in four health care settings. The average number of visits to mental health providers varied from 2.2 to 8.9 per patient and the percentage of visits by patients diagnosed as neurotic varied from 6.1% to 31.6%. The smaller the sample size used to develop expectations and the more divergent the target population is from this sample, the less appropriate are normative estimates.

Whether expectations for use of human services should be developed from epidemiologic surveys is debatable. The link between epidemiologic and social indicator predictors of problems and the actual use of services is weak and subject to multiple qualifications (Eaton, 1980; Taube, Lee, & Forthofer, 1984). Veroff et al. (1981) reports that only 3% of Americans seek professional help in time of crisis. National mental health services use rates of between 1% and 2% a year (Rosenstein & Milazzo-Sayre, 1981) are discrepant from epidemiologic estimates that between one in six and one in four Americans have serious mental problems. A series of large-scale epidemiologic surveys now under way (Eaton, Regier, Locke, & Taube, 1981) may provide a more accurate basis for epidemiologic estimates of use of services.

5.3 Professional Standards

Another source of expectations is professional standards found in many human service and educational programming areas. Although sometimes legally mandated, most standards have been developed by private accreditation agencies, for example, Commission on Accreditation of Rehabilitation Facilities (CARF). Table 5.4 presents service standards for community mental health centers from the Joint Commission on Accreditation of Hospitals (JCAH, 1979). The usefulness of a particular set of standards for estimating use depends on the extent to which the standards themselves were based on utilization experience.

5.4 Use Analysis

Use analysis combines expected use with analysis of actual clients seen and services provided by an agency or program. Information gathered to analyze use for a specific time period includes the following:

- client demographics, including place of residence. Unduplicated counts of new clients are the easiest to compare to target population descriptions.
- services provided. These allow computation and comparison of use rates for various categories of clients (demographic, diagnostic, cohort).
- referral source. These aid the study of barriers and facilitators of use.

Once this information is collected, use analysis could follow these four steps:

(1) Identify the percentage that each client subgroup makes up of the total client population. The subgroups used should be meaningful both locally and to funding sources.
(2) Compute rates of service used by each subgroup. Table 3.4 lists some issues in determining the measure (s) of service use. Examine these rates for deviations from the expectation that all groups will receive similar levels of services.
(3) Use target population information to compute use rates for client or treatment subgroups. Examine these rates for deviations from expectations. Expectation can be based on assumptions about representation in the target population (Section 4.5), the presence of at-risk characteristics (Section 4.3), the utilization experience of other agencies (Section 5.2), or professional standards (Section 5.3).
(4) If available, compute market share from a resource inventory (Section 3.2 and Exhibit 2.2).

Steps 1-4 will identify heavy-use groups, who currently use services and may be interested in using more services, and light-use groups, who may need additional or different services, or a different delivery system.

TABLE 5.4
Selected JCAH Staffing Standards for Accreditation
of Community Mental Health Centers,
Subprinciple 125.2

Case finding	3 staff per 1,000,000 population
Screening	2.3 staff per daily visit
Crisis intervention	4.5 staff per daily visit
Temporary residence	0.3 staff per resident
Remotivational care	0.7 staff per resident
Social training	0.125 staff per daily visit
Transitional living	0.2 staff per resident
On-site training	0.25 staff per daily visit
Patient/client education	0.125 staff per daily visit
Sustaining care	1.1 staff per resident
Case management	230 staff per 1,000,000 population
Dietary	Surveyor judgment[a]
Research and evaluation	7 staff per 1,000,000 population

a. Determined at time of site visit to agency by Accreditation team.

The final step in use analysis examines the delivery system for barriers that may inhibit or facilitate use of a program or service.

Barriers to Use

Analysis of discrepancy between expected and actual use does not lead directly to the inference of need because use is based on factors other than need:

Barriers	Physical, financial, and time constraints are greater for some groups;
Cultural variations	Subgroups perceive their own needs differently and find some solutions more acceptable than others;
Competition	Other agencies provide the same services and, especially in the human services, many "nonprofessional" alternatives exist.

Analyzing the importance of these factors requires information beyond utilization rates and population descriptions (Sorensen, Hammer, & Windle, 1979). Often a survey of relevant individuals must be conducted to discover barriers to use of services (Chapter 6).

One factor affecting use is *availability*, whether and how much of a service is offered. For many services, standard ratios, for example, the number of beds per 1000 citizens, exist to guide judgments of availability (Section 5.3). A resource inventory (Chapter 3) can be helpful in judging availability, although capacity is difficult to estimate. The link between availability and need is complicated by substitution (use of other services to meet a need), spillage, and seepage (Section 3.6).

A second factor is *awareness*:

- whether the client, or a significant other, recognizes a need, and
- whether the client or other knows that the service is available

In the first case, the person is unaware of the problem; in the second, the person is unaware that a solution is available. For many human services it is more important that well-placed people in the community are aware of a program (e.g., lawyers, school counselors) than that potential consumers are aware. Often examination of client's referral sources will gauge this second level of awareness.

A third factor affecting use is *acceptability*: whether a client would use a service if it were needed. Acceptability is determined by clients' attitudes toward the agency and the services it provides. Clients' attitudes are affected by the psychological cost of using the service. Many mental health and welfare services still carry a stigma that must be born by users. A survey of clients or potential consumers may be necessary to determine acceptability problems.

The fourth factor affecting utilization is *accessibility:* whether the costs of using a service are greater than the client is willing to bear. Costs include financial charges, physical discomforts, and procedural delays such as distance to travel, waiting time, and availability of child care. The distribution of clients over the area served by the agency (on a map, Section 10.3) can reveal problems of accessibility.

Use and Need

The relationship between use of services and need for service is complex. On the one hand economists (e.g., Frank, 1983) identify need with use of services and with the costs clients will bear to receive them. Although direct charges are not always relevant in education and human services, indirect charges sometimes are available. The greater the use of a service the more it is needed. Waiting lists, 100% occupancy, full classes, and endurance of delayed appointments indicate need. Unfortunately, market mechanisms do not exist in the human services and education to allow regular assessment of need on this basis.

On the other hand, nonuse of services may indicate comparative need. If a subgroup is similar on important characteristics to other groups that use a service, the expectation is that the subgroup would show similar use rates. However, accuracy of generalization of use may require field testing.

Finally, use may be unrelated to need. Services are only a solution. The inference of need requires not only a solution, but a problem and the expectation that the solution will modify the problem. Existence of a service may interfere with identification of a more effective or efficient solution.

5.5 Strengths and Weaknesses

The strength of use analysis comes from its emphasis on utilization of services. No agency can continue to fund programming that is not utilized. Depending on the quality of an agency's management information system, use analyses should be cheap and quick. However, there are several theoretical and practical problems with it. Use, by definition, is an indicator of the status quo. Examination of those who use services may tell little about those who do not use a service now, but might under other circumstances. Further, use patterns suffer the same problems of ecological fallacies as do social indicators and epidemiologic surveys (Section 4.3). Finally, predicting use is difficult. It depends on such factors as competition, substitution, and prediction of need. Many of the problems summarized in this section can be avoided if utilization information is supplemented with data from relevant populations, for example, nonusers. The use of surveys is discussed in the next chapter and qualitative data collection methods are described in Chapter 7.

EXERCISES

1. Compute utilization rates for the birth control counseling program of Exercise 3 of Chapter 4. Use the total number of students in each class and the number of at-risk students as denominators. Compare these estimates.

2. Estimate the number of admissions to mental health facilities for the place of your early childhood using the age and sex information from Exercise 1 of Chapter 4. Use the admission rates from Table 5.2 How does this estimate of need for services change over the 1960, 1970, and 1980 censuses?

3. Analyze barriers to use for a service in your town, for example, a swimming pool. Interview two people who use the service and two people who do not. Focus on either acceptability or accessibility. How important are these factors in separating users from nonusers?

6

Surveying Needs

Surveys are a popular method of gathering information on needs. They provide a flexible means of assessing the expectations both of subgroups of the target population and of other audiences to the need analysis. Specific issues concerning choice of method, question format, and use and coding of open-ended questions are discussed. Advantages, disadvantages, and procedures are presented for training, client, key informant, and citizen surveys. The development of large sample, technical surveys requires expert consultation and is discouraged.

We have a love affair with surveys. Surveys tell us how we think, feel, and act. Hardly a day goes by without a survey receiving prominent play on the evening news or in a newspaper editorial. In need analysis, the lure of the survey is just as strong. Surveys occur in a rich variety of scope, content, and length. They focus on problems, on solutions, on descriptions, and on forecasts.

Surveys provide a flexible means of assessing the expectation both of subgroups of the target population and of other audiences to the need analysis. Surveys can be designed to address problems of the specific target population and barriers to their use of services. Surveys are usually a necessary component for linking the problems revealed by social indicator analysis (Chapter 4) and solutions that will be acceptable to the target population (Section 5.4). Surveys can generate a great deal of information; they probe attitudes and opinions as well as measure behaviors and population characteristics. With expert consultation, surveys can also provide diagnostic information (however, see Section 6.8).

Surveys differ from data-gathering methods discussed in Chapters 4 and 5 because they involve people besides those conducting the need analysis. Surveys create the impression that problems identified will be addressed and that solutions examined will be implemented. Because surveys can engender enthusiasm or stir up trouble, their use adds another dimension to the decision to analyze needs: community awareness. This factor can be either positive or negative depending on the use made of the need analysis. Surveys have the potential to be expensive and complex. Because of this, generalization from existing data (e.g., synthetic estimation, Section 4.2) and group interview techniques such as those presented in Chapter 7 are often used as alternatives to surveys.

There are many excellent discussions of the conduct of surveys (Dillman, 1978; Fowler, 1984; Lockhart, 1984). This chapter discusses aspects of the survey process relevant to need analysis (Sections 6.1-6.3) as well as specific types of surveys (Sections 6.4-6.8). The choice of survey method, question format and wording, and use of open-ended questions are discussed. Training, client, key informant, and citizen surveys are presented.

6.1 Choice of Method

Three survey methods are usually considered for need analysis: face-to-face interviews, telephone interviews, and mailed surveys.

Interviews

The face-to-face interview allows for in-depth, person-to-person exchanges. It is the most appropriate of all survey methods for impaired or otherwise marginal members of society. Unfortunately, interviews are often prohibitively expensive. Costs of up to $30 a completed interview are common. Volunteer interviewers can be used but they will need extensive training and quality controls. Telephone interviews (Lavrakas, 1987) allow much of the personal contact of face-to-face interviews at a lower cost. When interviewers call from a single location, telephone surveys allow inexpensive monitoring of interviewer behavior.

Mailed Surveys

Mailed surveys provide a flexible method for gathering large samples of responses. Careful application of procedures similar to Dillman's (1978) will guarantee an adequate return rate. In some situations, rather than distribution by mail, questionnaires can be given to respondents at the time of contact with an agency.

Sampling

Surveys typically cover only a small sample of the population of interest. Many advances have been made in the use of representative sampling to allow accurate generalization to the population from the sample (Fowler, 1984). Accuracy is relevant when the purpose of the survey is to estimate the *frequency* of behaviors, attitudes, or beliefs in a larger population. Expert consultation is usually required to develop a representative sample.

In need analyses, surveys often have an additional or alternative purpose: revealing the *variety* of behaviors, attitudes, and beliefs of a target population. They seek variability rather than central tendency. When the range of responses is critical, purposive rather than representative sampling is best. For purposive sampling, specific representatives of subgroups are selected to participate. Purposive sampling is also best when the number of people to be sampled is limited, for example, by cost or time factors.

6.2 Question Format

Issues of question format that are particularly relevant to need analysis are the use of rankings versus ratings, controlling for social desirability of responses, and readability. Use and coding of open-ended responses is covered in the next section.

Ranking Versus Ratings

Need analysis surveys often ask respondents to choose among various alternatives, for example, possible programs that could be provided. Both ranking and rating formats are used to present the choices. Ratings are simpler for respondents, especially when the number of options is large, and allow application of advanced statistical techniques to develop an order of needs. Ratings allow respondents to express disinterest in all options whereas rankings require that some option be number 1. In its favor, a ranking format confronts the respondent with the basic question of many need analyses: how should various needs be ordered by importance? Questions formats like that shown in Table 6.1 combine both methods.

TABLE 6.1
Example of Combination Ranking
and Rating Question Format

Rating question:	A number of students have reported an interest in getting information on various issues related to sex and sexuality. I'm going to read you a list of these issues. Please tell me whether you have no, some, or very great interest in receiving information on this issue.
	A. Pregnancy and childbirth
	B. Improving communication with partner
	C. . . .
	K. Getting help for sexual problems
Ranking question:	I'll read you this list again and I'd like you to pick out the two issues that would be of greatest interest to you.

SOURCE: Adapted from McKillip & Kulp, 1985.
NOTE: Rank order of program options for ranking and rating questions correlated .84.

Social Desirability

Because need analyses concern growth or remedial programming, social desirability may affect survey responses. Respondents tend to overestimate the frequency or strength of popular behaviors, interests, or attitudes. Respondents find it difficult to admit lack of interest in training experiences. Second, respondents tend to underestimate the frequency or strength of unpopular behaviors, interests, or attitudes. Respondents are reluctant to admit to problems such as alcoholism, child abuse, or illiteracy.

Many solutions have been proposed to social desirability problems. Some, such as use of lie scales or repeating questions in the same survey, will be irritating or insulting to respondents. Sudman and Bradburn (1982) provide multiple suggestions for asking questions that might produce socially desirable responses:

(1) Use long, open-ended questions with words familiar to respondents for undesirable behavior.
(2) Ask informants about the behavior of others, for example, family or friends.
(3) Bias a question in favor of reporting undesirable behaviors and against reporting desirable behaviors.

(4) Precede questions about current undesirable behavior by asking if the behavior "ever" occurred. For socially desirable behavior ask about current *not* usual behavior.

(5) Embed threatening topics in a list of less threatening topics.

Readability

Because respondents to need analysis surveys often have low literacy levels, the readability of questions and directions will be important. Flesch (1960) gives the following formula for estimating reading ease:

$$\text{reading ease} = 206.835 - \left(\begin{array}{c}\text{average}\\ \text{sentence} \\ \text{length}\end{array} * 1.015\right) - \left(\begin{array}{c}\text{\# syllables}\\ \text{per 100} \\ \text{words}\end{array} * .846\right)$$

Table 6.2 gives interpretations of computed scores. If the typical respondent has less than a high school education, questionnaire text should not be more difficult than "standard."

6.3 Open-ended Questions

Need analysis surveys often ask respondents' opinions in an open-ended format. Using this format respondents are free to use their own terms and categories, without the imposition of a response system by the surveyor. The disadvantage is that responses must be coded into a limited number of categories before analysis can be done.

Asking Open-ended Questions

Open-ended questions, either in an interview or on a questionnaire, allow respondents to discuss or elaborate on their experiences, attitudes, or motives. Open-ended questions are particularly useful for probing and for generating ideas. Getting respondents to express themselves may be difficult. Patton (1980) suggests procedures to elicit the most useful answers:

(1) Questions should not suggest the dimension of response. Instead of "Did you find . . . helpful?" try "What was your feeling about . . .?" Instead of "Do you find that . . . causes you problems?" try "What do you think about . . . ?"

(2) Questions should presuppose that the respondent can give answers but should avoid using "why?" Instead of "Are there reasons people do not

TABLE 6.2
Interpretations of Reading Ease Scores,
Adapted from Flesch (1960)

Description of Style	Reading Ease Score
Very easy	90-100
Easy	80-90
Fairly easy	70-80
Standard	60-70
Fairly difficult	50-60
Difficult	40-50
Very difficult	0-30

use . . . ?" or "Why do people not use . . . ?", try "What kinds of barriers keep people from using . . . ?" Instead of "Can we make this service easier to use?" try "How can we make . . . ?"

(3) Ask one question at a time but do not ask questions that can be answered dichotomously. After reasons, likes, or barriers have been elicited, explore them individually with probes: "Say more about . . . ?" or "What do you mean by . . . ?"

(4) Let respondents use their own terms. They may use a different name or conceptualize a service at a different organizational level than does the questioner. Instead of "When did you first think about starting at XYZ university?" try "What program are you in? [response] When did you first think about starting [response] program?"

(5) Role-playing questions help respondents understand the type of information the surveyor is looking for. "Suppose I were new in town, how would I find out about . . . ?" or "Suppose I need medical care, where would you send me?"

Open-ended interviewing takes considerably more preparation and care than structured interviews. Response can lead to new questions as the interviewer seeks to understand the response. The interviewer must have a good understanding of the information that is needed or the interview will quickly wander from its focus. Fortunately many human service and education professionals have the experience and training to be able to use this technique.

Coding Open-ended Data

Once responses have been gathered they must be organized to allow analysis and summary. Holsti (1969) suggests criteria for constructing categories for coding responses to open-ended questions. Categories should

- reflect the purpose of the study, for example, types of services that might be provided, or problems that confront the respondent
- be exhaustive so that all responses can be placed in a category. Use of a miscellaneous category is typical. Categories with less than 5% of responses or more than 25% of responses should be redefined.
- be mutually exclusive so that no unit of response may be placed in more than one category. An individual answer may need to be broken into more than one unit for categorization.
- be independent so that assignment of a unit to a category does not affect assignment of other units. This requirement is not used when categories attempt to rank responses along a dimension, for example, favorableness.

A general procedure for developing categories involves these steps:

(1) typing transcripts of all open-ended answers, including an identification number if responses need to be related to other information gathered in the survey
(2) examining a portion of the answers to develop a tentative category system with characteristics described above. The unit of classification must be chosen. An individual answer might contain multiple units
(3) write a definition for each response category
(4) have another analyst examine another portion of answers with the tentative category system and revise as needed
(5) score all open-ended answers with the revised coding system

Final categorization of responses may be done by more than one analyst if reliability information is necessary. This is usually not required.

6.4 Training Surveys

Analysis of training needs is among the most frequent type of need analysis. Businesses, human service agencies, and educational institutions devote considerable resources to improving the skills of their employees. Misanchuk (1984) has identified three components of training need: the *competence* or ability of individuals to perform a task; the *relevance* of a skill or ability for the job role; and the individual's *desire* to undertake training. Most analyses of training needs have focused on the first two of these components. Using the schema of Table 6.3, training needs are confined to the quadrant defined by low current competence and high job relevance.

Surveys are used in training need analyses because respondents, usually potential trainees themselves, are expert enough to be able to diagnose the skills necessary for their jobs. A survey of the potential training population allows measurement of desire for training, as well as identifying training needs.

A training need survey follows these steps:

(1) A list of potential training topics is developed. This list may come from the work of a small committee of experts, for example, supervisors, or may be the result of a task analysis[1] for the job (Lauffer, 1982).
(2) A survey is developed asking respondents to rate each potential training topic
   - on the level of competence of current job holders (what is);
   - on the relevance of the training topic to the job (what should be); and
   - on current job holder's interest in the training topic (desire).
   Five point scales might be used ranging from low (1) to high (5). (See Exhibit 6.1)
(3) Training topics that get an average rating of greater than 3 on relevance and less than three on competence are identified as training needs. Exhibit 6.1 presents a method for making finer distinctions among these topics.
(4) Actual training topics are selected from training needs on the basis of respondents' desire for the training and of the cost of providing training on the topic

---

Exhibit 6.1
Assessing Training Needs

Cummings (1984) developed an approach to assessment of training needs that makes greater use of competence and relevance ratings than Table 6.3. He analyzed ratings of a training curriculum by 163 experts in accounting, tax consultation, and management information systems. A total of 25 content areas were rated on "the knowledge level that should exist for individuals who are working with construction industry clients" (relevance) and on "knowledge level that does exist for individuals who are working with construction industry clients" (competence). A five-point scale was used for both ratings, ranging from "almost none" (1) to "extensive" (5).

TABLE 6.3
Schema for Classifying Training Needs

Relevance of Task or Skill to Job	Current Competence at Task	
	High	*Low*
High		Training need
Low		

Arguing that distinctions among competence and relevance rankings should not be ignored (Misanchuk, 1984), Cummings (1984) assigned need values as shown in Table 6.4. Higher values indicated greater need for training in the area. For example, if a respondent indicated that the training topic was somewhat relevant to the job (4) and that most job members had little competence on the topic (2), need for training on the topic was scored as 2 for the respondent. If, on the other hand, the training topic was very relevant (5), need for training on the topic would be scored as 4. Topics that were rated below 3 on relevance or above 3 on competence were assigned a need value of 0. A weighted need index (WNI) was constructed for each training content area with this formula:

$$\text{WNI} = (\text{Sum over all cells } f_{ij} * V_{ij}) / N.$$
$$\text{in Table 6.4}$$

where f_{ij} is the number of respondents whose ratings fall in the cell ij, V_{ij} is the need value assigned to the cell in Table 6.4, N is the total number of respondents, i is the relevance rating, and j is the competence rating. WNI ranges from 0 (indicating no assessed need) to 5 (indicating maximum assessed need).

6.5 Client Surveys

Frequently surveys include current or former users of a service or program. This population is especially important because these respondents have had experience with the program and can evaluate its operation and barriers to its use (client satisfaction), and because they may be able to reflect on the motivation of users of the service (consumer choice). Also, consumers are usually available to program personnel

TABLE 6.4
Need Values for Cummings (1984)
Weighted Need Index

Relevance to Job	Current Competence at Task		
	3	2	1[a]
5[b]	3	4	5
4	1	2	4
3	0	1	3

a. "almost none."
b. "extensive."

and are more likely than nonconsumers to take the time to complete a survey.

Client Satisfaction

Surveys of consumer or client satisfaction are common in the human services and education. They bring an essential perspective to need analysis and serve to counter the absence of market mechanisms for evaluation and planning of services.

There are several drawbacks to the use of client satisfaction surveys, however. Some question the ability of clients to make valid discriminations between satisfactory and unsatisfactory programming, for example, students or mental health patients. Careful development research on client satisfaction measures has routinely resulted in scales that only measure gross satisfaction or dissatisfaction (Larsen, Attkisson, Hargreaves, & Nguyen, 1979; Smith, Falvo, McKillip, & Pitz, 1984). Judgments of components of programs are highly correlated with overall judgments. Larsen et al. (1979) found that the 3-item scale shown in Table 6.5 correlated highly with scores on a 31-item scale developed to cover nine components of mental health services.

A related issue is that client satisfaction ratings are invariably positive. In an examination of 26 consumer satisfaction studies in mental health, Lebow (1982) found that between 70% and 90% of respondents were "satisfied," and that a median of 49% of respondents were "very satisfied."

A third objection to consumer satisfaction surveys has to do with sampling bias. Because consumers, by definition, were aware of an available and accessible program, they differ from those impeded by a

TABLE 6.5
Three Item Client Satisfaction Questionnaire,
Adapted from Larsen et al. (1979)

1. To what extent has our program met your needs?

_____Almost all of my needs have been met.

_____Most of my needs have been met.

_____Only a few of my needs have been met.

_____None of my needs have been met.

2. In an overall, general sense, how satisfied are you with the services you have received?

_____Very satisfied

_____Mostly satisfied

_____Indifferent or mildly dissatisfied

_____Quite dissatisfied

3. If you were to seek help again, would you come back to our program?

_____No, definitely not

_____No, I do not think so

_____Yes, I think so

_____Yes, definitely

lack of information. Consumers who respond to the survey may not represent all consumers, but may represent an oversample of the more satisfied (Ellsworth, 1979). Finally, consumers surveys, especially when distributed at the time of service use, are potentially reactive. Respondents say what they think their teachers or therapists want to hear.

If agency personnel really want useful satisfaction information, Larsen et al. (1979) gives these recommendations to increase the usefulness of consumer surveys:

(1) Focus on dissatisfaction, through use of open-ended questions and by examination of relative satisfaction.
(2) Examine satisfaction trends over time.
(3) Include specific questions about barriers to service.

Consumer Choice

Kotler (1982) provides a five-stage model of consumer choice that is useful for need analysis. The model examines the process consumers follow in making use of a service. The first stage in consumer choice is *need arousal*, where consumers develop initial interest. Factors triggering interest may be a friend, an incident, or a media report. Human services and education often rely on gatekeepers in the community to make referrals. It may be important to examine the aspects of the service that arouse consumers' or gatekeepers' interest.

The second stage in consumer choice is *information gathering*. Important aspects of this stage are the amount and source of information that consumers consult after their initial interest is aroused. Both customer characteristics and type of service will affect information gathering.

The third stage of choice is *decision evaluation*. It may be important for an agency to know the alternatives potential consumers consider before choosing to use the service. Examination of alternatives reveals the need that consumers are satisfying by their choice. Some consumers consider few alternatives before making a choice while others do not use the service until several alternatives have been investigated and found wanting.

The fourth stage of choice is *decision execution*. Here it is important to examine factors that facilitate or inhibit use of service once a decision has been made. Common factors are the opinion of significant others and aspects of the initial contact. Difficulty in parking or a brusque exchange with a receptionist may frustrate use. Cultural acceptability and the support of others facilitate use. The final stage in choice is *postdecisional assessment*, which is closely tied to consumer satisfaction.

Analysis of the choice behavior involved in use of a service might use client surveys, key informant surveys, or more qualitative techniques (Chapter 7).

6.6 Key Informant Surveys

Key informants are opportunistically connected individuals with the knowledge and ability to report on community needs. Key informants are lawyers, judges, physicians, ministers, minority group leaders, and service providers who are aware of the needs and services perceived as important by a community. Key informant surveys are quick and relatively inexpensive to conduct. They are particularly useful when the problems investigated are rare, and when issues of acceptability of a service are raised. Because they are important members of their communities, surveying key informants may affect community support for program changes. On the negative side, key informants have an organizational perspective on community needs and a bias toward the activities in which each is involved. Key informant reports will often overestimate problems facing the target population and underestimate the population's ability to solve these problems. Exhibit 6.2 presents two examples of these biases.

Key informants should be chosen to cover the full range of community opinion. In some situations, political and geographic balance among informants is important. Hagedorn (1977) suggests that a sample of 10-15 is adequate for this type of survey. A combination of mailed or phone prenotice that includes an outline of questions to be asked and face-to-face interviews will maximize the information and good will gained. Questions should cover both general and specific needs of the target population, as well as issues of accessibility and acceptability of solutions. Characteristics of the informants should also be gathered, such as institutional affiliation and experience with the target population.

Exhibit 6.2
Comparison of Key Informant
and Citizen Surveys for
Measuring Health Behaviors

Deaux and Callaghan (1984) compared estimates of the prevalence of health-risk behaviors for residents of the state of New Mexico. Mailed survey responses from 213 key informants were compared to those from telephone interviews with 816 randomly selected residents of the state. Table 6.6 presents results for some of the behaviors examined. Key informants consistently gave higher estimates of health-risk behaviors than did the resident survey. Key informants also underestimated health promotion behaviors.

Deaux and Callaghan (1985) present evidence that raises questions about the validity of both surveys. Key informants estimated that 20% of the state's residents always or nearly always used seat belts, and 27% of residents similarly classified themselves. Observations by the New Mexico Department of Transportation during the time of the survey indicated that only 11% of that state's residents used seat belts! Workman (1980) compared estimates of the interest of married students at a large midwestern university in ten programs aimed at reducing stress. Key informant interviews yielded estimates of definite

TABLE 6.6
Comparison of Key Informant and Citizen Survey Estimates
of Citizen Health Behaviors

Behavior	Key Informant Survey	Citizen Survey
Overweight	50	30
DWI in the past four weeks	23	7
Average percentage of cigarettes smoked per week	94	41
Active sports participation, times per month	2.3	10.5
Always or nearly always wear seat belts	20	27

SOURCE: Adapted from Deaux & Callaghan (1984).
NOTE: Figures reflect percentages.

interest" among residents averaging 46%. Telephone interviews of residents showed an average of 25% definite interest in the same programs ($t(9)$ = 3.61, $p < .01$). Levels of estimated interest were correlated, however ($r(9)$ = .85).

6.7 Citizen Surveys

Citizen surveys seek to overcome objections that client and key informant samples give too restricted or biased estimates of the needs and desires of the target population. Residents of broad geographical areas or individuals on an organization's membership list are polled on a random or representative basis. Most of these surveys seek to determine citizens' impressions of the seriousness of problems or the acceptability of solutions. A school district may ask residents' opinions about the quality of education or city administration may seek to estimate support for mass transit or public works. Such surveys seek to duplicate on a local level the function played by large sample surveys for policy makers on the federal or state level. The primary problems with citizen surveys are the complexity and cost of execution and analysis. Rarely can an individual agency mount a citizen survey without outside consultants. Probably even more rarely does the information gained justify the cost and effort involved. Most of the information available through citizen surveys can be obtained with other survey techniques discussed in this chapter or by a qualitative technique presented in Chapter 7.

Occasionally, agencies will mount a citizen survey not just to gauge citizen opinions but also to diagnose a target population's problems. Epidemiologic surveys serve this latter function. Some (e.g., Schwab, 1983) consider such surveys to have the "greatest scientific merit" of all techniques of need identification. Others (e.g., Dunham, 1983) judge that it is "almost impossible to conduct meaningful epidemiologic investigations." Mounting an epidemiologic survey is difficult and complex.

6.8 Observations

Epidemiologic surveys provide an example of an "observational" method of need analysis. For these methods, outcomes of the target population are measured directly rather than indirectly through self-reports or the reports of others. Some social indicators (e.g., crime rates) are observational measures. Other examples are task analysis, standardized tests, and psychodiagnostic tests. In contrast to the methods of assessing needs presented in Chapter 3-7, observational methods are usually highly technical and situation-specific. Where available, the results of direct observations of the target population's outcomes play a crucial role in determining their status. Most of the techniques reviewed in chapters 3-7 assume that direct observational information is not available or relevant. Like epidemiologic surveys, most observational techniques are complicated and require expert consultation.

6.9 Strengths and Weaknesses

Conducting surveys is a popular planning activity that brings with it credibility. Surveys can often yield useful data for need identification and assessment. They allow direct feedback from clients, key informants, and target populations about specific issues raised in a need analysis. Surveys can help develop public awareness of problems and build a consensus for solutions. Surveys do not suffer problems of across-level inferences that affect other techniques. Among the disadvantages of surveys are their potential complexity and expense. They often yield information on *wants* rather than *needs* and can only be used cautiously to predict actual utilization. Finally, surveys are reactive. They can arouse expectations among respondents that action is about to be taken. Much that can be gained by a large sample survey is available with the techniques discussed in the next chapter or by extrapolation from existing information.

EXERCISES

1. Examine the readability of promotional material available from a human service or education agency in your town. How does it reading-ease score compare with what is known about the population the material is intended to reach?

2. Conduct a survey of ten people about barriers they have encountered using a service available in your town. Use open-ended questions and develop a category system for analyzing the responses.

3. Interview three people about the five consumer choice steps in their use of a public service. Were all steps relevant for each person?

NOTE

1. Assuming, of course, that the results of the task analysis were not sufficient to determine training needs.

7

Structured Groups

Structured groups provide a supplement and an alternative to surveys, social indicator analyses, and use analyses. Structured groups can give "qualitative" information to balance and test "quantitative" findings. Detailed steps for execution of focused groups, nominal groups, and delphi panels are presented, as is the role of the more public, political techniques of community forums and public hearings. The possibility of substituting these techniques for the more quantitatively oriented procedures reviewed in previous chapters is highlighted.

Perhaps the simplest method of need analysis is to assemble a group of experts and concerned citizens and charge them with identifying the needs of the population served by the agency. Using their knowledge and experience with the population and the services available, a need analysis committee can identify problems and their solutions. That such a straightforward approach is often unsuccessful is testified to by the wide variety of structured-group techniques presented in this chapter.

Structured groups provide a supplement and an alternative to the need identification techniques reviewed in previous chapters (Moore, 1987). *Focused groups* are widely used in marketing to explore consumers' reactions to products or packaging. They can be used in need identification to explore the acceptability and accessibility of proposed solutions, or to test hypotheses generated from social indicator or use analysis. Focused groups serve both as an alternative and as supplement to survey techniques. *Nominal groups* provide a highly structured, but interactive, way to generate and evaluate ideas. They are useful for identifying problems of a target population and generating solutions. A *delphi* panel is a forecasting technique useful for long-term projections and for evaluation of unusual or innovative interventions. It can be used to predict utilization, especially when there is little experience to guide projections. *Community forums and public hearings* are the data collection methods of choice in the political arena. They are useful when public display is critical to the acceptance of the results of a need analysis.

7.1 Focused Groups

Focused groups are used by market researchers to gauge consumers' reactions to products, both marketed and planned (Calder, 1977; Cox, Higginbotham, & Burton, 1976). Marketing personnel use focused groups to provide themselves with an opportunity to "hear consumers speak." Such opportunities may be particularly useful when those identifying and assessing needs are not members of the target population. The group setting in which participants discuss feelings and beliefs about their needs offers a dynamic environment to probe consumers' perspectives and to test researcher's understanding. The interaction of participants provides a unique source of information and serves to check the validity of one another's reactions. Components of a focused group are

(1) single or dual moderators with responsibility for leading the discussion. The moderator should be knowledgeable about the problem or the solution being examined, especially of results of social indicator (Chapter 4) or use analysis (Chapter 5). The moderator's job is to get participants to focus on their feelings and beliefs about various aspects of the program being considered. The moderator allows participants to respond in their own terms (Section 6.3), and uses probes to elicit more specific information.

(2) eight to ten participants selected to represent the target population or subgroup. Purposive rather than representative sampling is important (Section 6.2). Groups must be homogeneous enough to allow free interaction of members. Equal social status is usually required.

(3) sessions, lasting for 90 minutes. Participants are encouraged to be creative and express feelings as well as ideas. All members of the group are encouraged to participate. Provisions for recording the sessions are often made. Interaction between participants is encouraged.

Exhibit 7.1 presents an example of the use of focused groups in need analysis.

Focused groups provide the target population's perspective on needs. They are similar to surveys, especially open-ended interviews. Grouping of participants allows for quicker data collection than does individual interviews, although observations are not independent. What one member of a group says affects the reactions of others. If the results of focused groups are at variance with expectations based on other need identification techniques, additional data collection may be required, for example, a survey of the target population. The number of focused groups necessary for confidence in the results of this technique depends on the purpose of the need analysis and the degree of consensus of participants.

Exhibit 7.1
Use of a Focused Group
in Need Analysis

Long (1983) reports on the use of focused groups to help design a community-level coping-skills workshop for elderly residents. A total of five, one-hour focused groups were conducted with established groups of elderly people active at a senior citizens center. A discrepancy model was used to study the perceived need for the elderly to acquire new coping skills. Participants were questioned about changes that older people experience and problems caused by these changes (performance deficits). They were then asked what information and coping skills would have helped them ease the changes (solutions). Next, each group was asked to group the solutions. Sessions were ended with a check for unmentioned problems and satisfaction with priorities that the group had developed.

On the basis of the groups, four categories of educational needs were developed:

- preparation for change
- decision making and problem solving
- self-awareness
- personal support systems

The largest performance deficit was in the area of self-awareness. Consistency across focused groups in their identification of deficits and solutions was used to select the topics covered in the workshop.

7.2 Nominal Groups

Structured group processes are often used to overcome common problems of group dynamics: a few higher-status members do most of the talking, idea evaluation discourages idea generation, and groups stray from their agenda. Delbecq (1983; Moore, 1987) developed the nominal group technique to allow for idea generation and evaluation while avoiding problems of group dynamics. Clients, key informants, citizens, or service providers are assembled to identify problems or to propose solutions. Nominal groups can be assembled specially for the need analysis or may be those attending regular staff meetings. Nominal groups generally take between two and four hours.

The technique requires a room large enough to hold all participants, tables for every 6-9 participants; a flip pad for each table, and paper or index cards. The steps for running a nominal group include the following:

(1) Develop questions for participants requiring that they generate problem dimensions or differentiated solutions, for example, what factors account for a high rate of teenage preganancy in an area, or what alternatives are available for promoting responsible student alcohol use.

(2) Participants should be selected from those who can contribute to answering the questions that have been developed. Representatives of different perspectives should be included in the total group and in the subgroups of 6-9 members at each table. A leader should be identified at each table.

(3) After subgroups have been assembled and the full procedure described to all participants, each participant should answer the first question by writing individual alternatives on index cards. Discussion is not permitted at this step.

(4) Ideas generated are recorded on a flip chart in round-robin fashion. Each participant presents one idea in turn until all ideas have been listed. Discussion is not allowed.

(5) Each idea is explained and clarified but not criticized or collapsed with others. No more than 25% of the time allowed for the entire process should be expended on this step.

(6) Each group member privately ranks the top ideas on index cards, for example, the top five. These cards are handed in and the popularity of the ideas are recorded on the flip chart.

(7) A brief clarifying discussion is held. Surprise rankings may be due to misunderstandings of ideas.

(8) Each member again privately ranks the top ideas. Rankings from subgroups are combined for an overall tally.

(9) The cycle is repeated for each of the questions.

The result of the nominal group is a priority ranking of answers to various need analysis questions. The validity of the answers may need to be tested by other need identification techniques. Exhibit 7.2 presents an example of the use of nominal groups in need analysis.

Exhibit 7.2
Use of a Nominal Group
in Energy Planning

Roitman (1981) used nominal groups to help develop a community energy plan for a moderate-size community in Michigan. A total of 39 individuals from 104 invited organizations participated. These questions were raised:

- What do you see as the major needs of the [geographic] area with regard to energy conservation programs and services?
- What problems do you think people are running into when they actually try to conserve energy?

Following the nominal group procedure, participants first answered these questions individually and then discussed their answers in small groups. Discussions involved round-robin listing of ideas, clarification of these ideas, and then, ranking of the ideas.

Table 7.1 presents Roitman's categorization of the ideas generated. Awareness ideas (Category 1) received the greatest number of rankings (from step 8 of the procedure). Roitman reports that the distribution of ideas among categories and importance rankings was nearly identical to the results of a key informant survey of sixty people from the 104 organizations invited to participate in the nominal groups.

7.3 Delphi Panels

Delphi panels provide an intuitive approach to forecasting[1] that is useful when past experience is weak or conflicting (Lauffer, 1982; Linstrom & Turoff, 1975). The procedure is flexible and combines anonymous gathering of quantitative estimates, feedback to respondents, and the opportunity to alter responses because of the feedback. Estimates of the prevalence of a problem, of use of a service, and of impacts of a program provide examples of potential uses in need analysis. Delphi studies follow these procedures:

(1) A questionnaire is constructed concerning the forecasting question, for example, predicted use of a service by various subgroups of the target population. All questions require a numeric answer.
(2) The questionnaire is distributed to and completed by a panel of experts.

TABLE 7.1
Distribution of Energy Conservation Ideas
Generated by Nominal Groups

Category	Needed Programs	Problems
Information, knowledge, awareness, and belief	43	73
Planning, regulation, coordination, leadership, and political action	59	52
Incentives to encourage conservation, cost of conservation efforts	18	51
Physical fixes, buildings, vehicles, and appliances	2	7
Lifestyle changes	1	12

(3) Responses are analyzed and the distribution of responses is developed for each question, for example, a median and interquartile range.

(4) A second questionnaire is distributed to the panel asking the same questions. With each question is the distribution of responses and the respondent's original answer. The respondent is given the opportunity to alter the answer and is asked for reasons to support an answer outside the interquartile range.

(5) These responses are analyzed; new distributions are developed and arguments for deviant responses are collected.

(6) A third questionnaire is distributed to the panel with new distributions, their current judgments, and the arguments for judgments higher and lower than the norm. They are given the opportunity to alter their responses and to list additional arguments for nonnormative responses.

(7) The procedure continues until those conducting the survey are satisfied with the narrowness of the forecasts developed or until panelists no longer alter their responses.

7.4 Public Forums

Community forums (town meetings) and public hearings are data-gathering techniques from the political arena. Both afford public presentation and evaluation of the need analysis, a factor important in engendering public support and overcoming public skepticism.

Public Hearings

Public hearings are an investigative and evaluative tool. Members of a committee hear testimony from selected witnesses, raise questions, cross-examine witnesses, and issue a summary report (St. John, 1984).

Public hearings are appropriate when the impact of the need analysis is dependent on consensus of multiple perspectives and consensus requires significant interaction among the parties. Hearings are also useful when the need analysis takes place in a politicized atmosphere in which advocates of one perspective or another are likely to dismiss its findings. "Blue-ribbon" committees can increase the public credibility of a need analysis and calm concern over its implications, at least in the short run.

St. John identifies these steps in establishing and conducting hearings:

(1) The parent body, for example, a United Way board, outlines the charge to the committee, selects committee members, appoints a chair person, and identifies counsel and other professional support staff. The inclusion of representatives of affected groups, as well as experts from outside the management structure, will increase credibility.

(2) In line with the committee's charge, committee members and support staff prepare background work, brief other committee members, and identify witnesses.

(3) Plan the hearing, including notifying witnesses and informing them about the rules of operation.

(4) Conduct the hearing, including examination of witnesses. Credibility is in large part dependent on the seriousness of the hearing and the attention, reflected in questions, paid to the witnesses (Stenzel, 1982).

(5) Chairperson and counsel draft a report that is reviewed by other committee members. The final report is submitted to the parent body.

Community Forums

A less expensive but more public approach is a community forum or town meeting (Hagedorn, Beck, Neubert, & Werlin, 1976). Forums are used more to build support than to counter skepticism. They can be useful if a cross-section of the community is involved, if an experienced leader is available, and if the purpose of the forum is made clear.

A typical forum involves an evening meeting in a politically neutral auditorium. Concerned members of a community address need analysis issues such as desirability of a particular type of programming. Wide advertising is important, as are established group rules about the length and content of public statements. Rules, such as a 3-minute limit on statements, should be made explicit at the beginning of the forum and enforced by the leader. The purpose of the forum should be made clear by banners and frequently reiterated by the leader. Follow-up mailings thanking those who attended and summarizing the results (especially future actions) of the forum are important. A sign-up sheet collecting the names and addresses of participants will ease this task and provide the basis of assembling a network of interested community members.

7.5 Strengths and Weaknesses

Although the techniques reviewed in this chapter are diverse, they share strengths and weaknesses. First, they involve people. Involvement is a reflection of interest and a spur to commitment. Most of the group techniques can aid acceptance of the need analysis by key community and target population members. Commitment, however, brings with it the expectation of action. Techniques of this chapter should be avoided if the possibility of action is remote.

Many of the techniques discussed in this chapter are normally associated with "qualitative" rather than "quantitative" research methods (Filstead, 1979; Smith, 1983). Being qualitative, they impose fewer restrictions on the concepts and dimensions that participants use in describing their perceptions and judgments than do the more structured quantitative methods. Because they sometimes substitute for quantitative methods (e.g., surveys or use analyses), issues of *bias* are often raised for qualitative procedures. Though a satisfactory solution to this issue is still wanting, work is being done on it (e.g., Guba, 1981). As discussed in the next chapter (see also Section 1.2), all need analysis techniques have biases. Through careful combination of techniques, biases can be balanced. Human service and education personnel will often be more familiar with the techniques outlined in this chapter than those discussed in previous chapters and thus be more, rather than less, aware of potential biases.

EXERCISES

1. Use the nominal group technique to generate questions for an exam on a chapter of this text. Compare these questions on difficulty and appropriateness with those actually used by the instructor.

2. Attend a public hearing or community forum. Note methods used by the chairperson to keep the group on task.

3. Use a focused group to examine the five steps of consumer choice for use of a service in your town. Compare results with those of the face-to-face interviews (Exercise 3, Chapter 6).

NOTE

1. Delphi panels can also be used for generating and evaluating ideas in much the same manner as nominal groups (Moore, 1987).

8

Choosing Among Methods

Use of multiple methods of identifying needs allows for increased accuracy and decreased bias. However, the use of multiple methods increases the cost and complexity of the needs analysis. The strengths and weaknesses of need identification methods, along with the purposes of the analysis and the resources available for it, should be considered when selecting methods. A matrix is presented containing ratings of 22 need identification techniques on 14 attributes that are important to the choice of methods. The use of this matrix for selecting methods is discussed. Algorithms for identifying problems and solutions are presented.

It is almost axiomatic in discussions of data-gathering techniques in the need analysis literature to "never use one when two will do" (Steadham, 1980, p. 60). Siegel et al. (1978, p. 221) advocate *convergent analysis*, a "stepwise, multilevel, multitechnique" strategy. The key to need identification in convergent analysis is the choice of multiple but complementary methods for finding and describing needs. When possible, the methods should represent different perspectives on needs, for example, that of the target population and that of service providers. This chapter discusses the choice of need identification techniques. Chapter 9 presents a model for integrating the results of multiple need identification techniques.

8.1 Using Multiple Methods

A driving idea in the development of research methods over the last 30 years has been triangulation, the notion that measurement of a construct (e.g., need) requires more than one instrument (e.g., Campbell & Fiske, 1959; Crano, 1981). Any one method is assumed to present a unique, but imperfect, perspective on the need of the target population. One method measures need only partially. Using more than one method can identify need more fully. In addition, every method taps factors irrelevant to need. Each has its own biases. Strategic selection of need identification methods can weaken biases and more fully and accurately reveal need.

One source of bias is the outcome expectation (Section 1.2) used to recognize need. For example, client surveys (Section 6.5) emphasize felt need and use analysis (Chapter 5) emphasizes expressed need. Felt need depends on the expectation the target population has for its own outcomes. Expressed need depends on programs currently available. Biases are minimized when methods use different outcome expectations. A second source of bias is the source of the information. Key informants have one perspective and community residents have another. Neither is without bias. Again, bias is minimized when the groups surveyed have different perspectives. Need is best identified by a combination of methods with differing outcome expectations and differing study populations.

Triangulation is not a panacea, however. Need analysis is not an end in itself but a tool of decision making. This applied focus suggests that need analysis is a "satisficing" activity, an action taken in order just to meet a minimal standard (Cummings & Bramlett, 1984). Because data collection and analysis is expensive, it ends at the point that the decision maker has just enough information to make the judgments that need to be made. The role of need analysis in decision making suggests a serial rather than parallel process for need identification. A data-gathering method is selected and used, results are analyzed, and a decision is made whether to collect additional information. If more information is needed, the process iterates (see Section 1.1).

8.2 Identification Method Attribute Matrix

Table 8.1 presents fourteen attributes of the need identification methods covered in Chapters 3-7. These attributes can serve as criteria for chossing between methods. In the table, each of the methods has been given a five-point rating on each attribute, from very characteristic (++), to very uncharacteristic (--). A "0" rating indicates a middle position. Though it is impossible to assign ratings that will be valid for all analyses, populations, and circumstances, the ratings in the table will serve as a guide. When choosing a method, not all criteria will be important. Only those attributes important for the choice of method should be considered. Each attribute is discussed below.

Resources

(1) *Low Cost.* Generally, library research and use of standards are the least expensive means of need identification, and large surveys and public hearings are the most expensive.

(2) *Short Time.* Surveys generally will take more time than other methods of need identification, followed by structured groups and then use of preexisting data, for example, social indicators.

(3) *Skill Needed.* Ratings are negatively correlated with those for low cost and short time. However, human service and education professionals should have little difficulty with basic uses of preexisting data, simple surveys, or interviews. Large community surveys and public hearings may require extensive outside consultation.

Analysis

(4) *Flexible.* Most methods of need analysis are flexible. For social indicators or resource inventories, needed data may not exist. Some structured-group techniques prescribe procedures that may not be adaptable.

(5) *Problem Orientation.* Social area and risk factor analyses, barrier analysis, and surveys of key informants are likely to yield information that emphasizes problems of the target population.

(6) *Solution Orientation.* Usually, techniques that help identify problems add little to identification of solutions. Structured groups may be useful for suggesting solutions. Because barrier analysis concerns problems with the delivery system (i.e., solutions), it may be doubly useful.

(7) *Relevance.* Ratings reflect relevance of the information gathered to the immediate situation. Lack of relevance may be caused by the need to generalize over levels of analysis, for example social area analysis, or the assumptions that problems will develop (e.g., risk factor analysis). Observations and use analysis have the greatest relevance to the immediate situation.

(8) *Credibility.* Ratings reflect the popularity or face validity of the data. Though social indicator analysis and synthetic estimation depend on the same logical processes, census data is given greater credibility than projections from other types of surveys. Some will question the credibility of "qualitative" as compared to "quantitative" methods of need identification.

(9) *Detail.* Some methods allow examination of fine distinctions and detailed probing, for example, public hearings and focused groups,

though others only yield gross generalizations, for example, social area analysis.

(10) *Ideas.* Library research, service provider interviews, focused groups, and nominal groups provide the best means of generating ideas for further investigation.

Audiences

(11) *Stakeholders.* Stakeholders are groups or individuals with an interest in the results of the need analysis. Some techniques allow them to participate and provide input for the analysis. Service professionals and agency clients are usually important stakeholders.

(12) *Interest.* Surveys and community forums serve both to measure and to increase the interest of participants in the need analysis. Depending on the analysis, community interest can be either a help or a hindrance.

Compatibility with Other Methods

(13) *Prerequisites.* Some methods are basic to the analysis (e.g., target population description) and others require ground work to have been done (e.g., client analysis).

(14) *Overlap.* Surveys, social indicators, and structured groups can substitute for each other. Substitutes for use analysis are not as available.

For example, needs are often identified by a social indicator analysis. Table 8.1 indicates that this technique would be relatively simple to do (low cost, short time, low skill needed, few prerequisites), would be credible, and would yield information about problems. As drawbacks, social indicator analysis is not a good technique for generating details or ideas, for yielding information on solutions, or for involving audiences to the need analysis. By comparison, a client survey would be more complicated, would yield detail and ideas, and would involve an important audience. The best single or combination of methods for need identification depends on the goals of the analysis and on the resources available.

8.3 Algorithms for Identifying Problems and Solutions

Identification of problems and solutions presumes information about the target population and the services available to them. Figures

TABLE 8.1
Need Identification Method Matrix

Attributes for Choosing between Methods

Need Identification Methods	Resources				Analysis		
	Low Cost	Short Time	Skill Needed	Flexible	Problem Oriented	Solution Oriented	Relevant
1. Resource Inventory (3.1 & 3.2)	-	-	-	0	--	++	-
2. Target Population Description (4.2)	+	+	-	+	+	-	+
3. Library Research (4.1)	++	+	-	++	+	+	0
4. Synthetic Estimation (4.2)	+	+	-	+	+	-	-
5. Social Area Analysis (4.2)	+	+	+	+	++	--	--
6. Risk Factor Analysis (4.3)	+	+	-	+	++	--	-
7. Social Indicator Analysis (4.4)	+	+	-	+	+	0	-
8. Client Analysis (4.5)	+	+	0	+	0	0	+
9. Use Analysis (5.2 & 5.4)	+	+	0	+	-	+	++
10. Barrier Analysis (5.4)	-	-	+	++	++	++	++
11. Standards (5.3)	++	++	--	-	+	+	--
12. Epidemiologic Survey (5.2 & 6.7)	--	--	++	++	+	+	+
13. Training Survey (6.4)	-	-	-	+	-	+	0
14. Key Informant Survey (6.6)	-	-	+	++	++	+	+
15. Client/Consumer Survey (6.5)	-	-	-	++	+	-	-
16. Citizen Survey (6.7)	--	-	++	++	+	+	++
17. Observation (6.8)	-	-	+	++	+	+	++
18. Focused Group (7.1)	+	0	-	++	+	+	+
19. Nominal Group (7.2)	+	0	-	0	+	++	0
20. Delphi Panel (7.3)	+	0	+	0	+	+	-
21. Public Hearing (7.4)	--	-	+	+	+	0	+
22. Community Forum (7.4)	+	0	+	+	+	-	0

NOTE: Numbers in parentheses are sections in which methods are discussed. Cell entries range from ++, indicating a criterion very characteristic of the method, to --, indicating a criterion very uncharacteristic of the method.

TABLE 8.1 (Continued)
Need Identification Method Matrix

	Attributes for Choosing between Methods						
	Analysis (Continued)			Audiences		Compatibility	
Need Identification Methods	Credibility	Detail	Ideas	Stakeholder	Interest	Prerequisites	Overlap
1. Resource Inventory (3.1. & 3.2)	++	0	–	+	+	–	–
2. Target Population Description (4.2)	+	+	+	–	–	–	–
3. Library Research (4.1)	0	+	++	–	–	–	–
4. Synthetic Estimation (4.2)	0	–	–	–	–	+	+
5. Social Area Analysis (4.2)	+	–	–	–	–	–	+
6. Risk Factor Analysis (4.3)	+	–	–	–	–	+	+
7. Social Indicator Analysis (4.4)	++	–	–	–	–	–	+
8. Client Analysis (4.5)	+	0	+	–	–	++	–
9. Use Analysis (5.2 & 5.4)	++	+	+	+	–	0	–
10. Barrier Analysis (5.4)	0	+	+	+	+	++	–
11. Standards (5.3)	0	+	+	–	–	–	+
12. Epidemiologic Survey (5.2 & 6.7)	+	+	+	0	+	–	+
13. Training Survey (6.4)	++	+	+	+	+	0	+
14. Key Informant Survey (6.6)	+	+	++	++	+	–	+
15. Client/Consumer Survey (6.5)	+	+	+	++	+	–	+
16. Citizen Survey (6.7)	+	0	0	0	++	–	+
17. Observation (6.8)	+	+	+	–	–	–	+
18. Focused Group (7.1)	0	++	++	–	–	–	+
19. Nominal Group (7.2)	0	+	++	+	0	–	+
20. Delphi Panel (7.3)	+	+	+	–	–	–	+
21. Public Hearing (7.4)	+	++	+	++	+	+	+
22. Community Forum (7.4)	0	–	–	++	++	+	+

NOTE: Numbers in parentheses are sections in which methods are discussed. Cell entries range from ++, indicating a criterion very characteristic of the method, to – –, indicating a criterion very uncharacteristic of the method.

8.1 and 8.2, which present algorithms for identifying problems and solutions, respectively, presume that the target population and its current services are known.

Figure 8.1 presents an algorithm for identifying problems. The first step in the process is to make expectations explicit. The analysis may assume that subgroups should be served in proportion to their representation in an at-risk population. A social indicator analysis would reveal the distribution of the at-risk population among the subgroups. The next step is to identify actual outcomes. A client analysis would show the actual use of services by the subgroups. Problems are revealed by discrepancies. Discrepancy occurs between expectations and

- actual outcomes,
- outcomes that a population will develop without action, and
- outcomes that a population will develop if action is withdrawn.

After discrepancies have been identified, solutions should be identified for each. If solutions are not desired, "need" identification has been completed and the analysis moves to needs assessment.

Figure 8.2 presents an algorithm for identifying solutions. It is assumed that before needs assessment takes place, a single best solution is identified for each problem. This is not always so. Problems might first be selected for intervention and then solutions identified and selected. Alternatively, solutions may be identified for funding, and then populations with problems identified. Problems and solutions may also be identified in a recursive manner; examination of solutions may lead to a deeper understanding of a problem that dictates a different solution.

When problems have been identified by comparison of social indicator and client analyses, solutions could be identified by a barrier analysis or by a key informant survey. Proposed solutions should be examined for cost, impact, and feasibility before solutions are paired with problems. Once this pairing is accomplished, need identification is completed. Figures 8.1 and 8.2 end with statements to proceed to needs assessment. Needs assessment models are discussed in Chapters 2 and 9.

EXERCISES

1. What method of need identification would best complement a social area analysis? Use Table 8.1 to justify your answer.

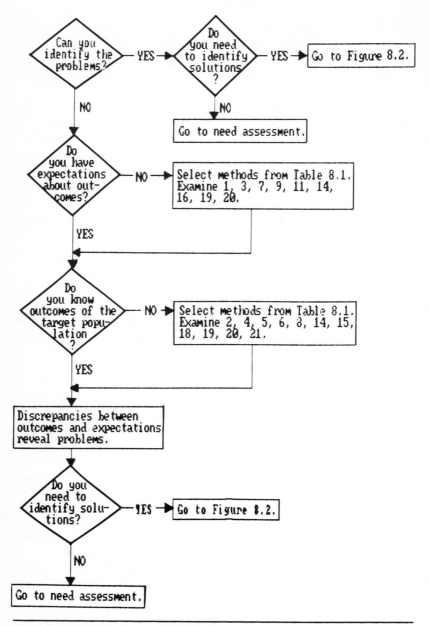

Figure 8.1 Algorithm for Identifying Problems

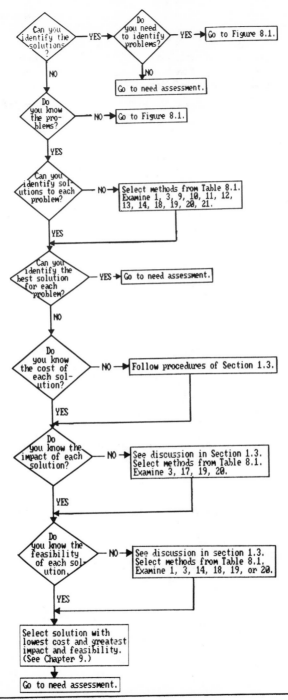

Figure 8.2   Algorithm for Identifying and Selecting Solutions

2. Apply Table 8.1 to the methods of need identification used in a published need analysis. Where is the analysis strong? Weak? What single additional method would have done the most to strengthen the analysis?

3. Use the algorithm of Figure 8.2 to select methods of identifying solutions to problems identified in the barrier analysis of Exercise 2 of Chapter 6. What information would you need to gather?

NOTE

1. Section 4.3 reviews four methods frequently used to estimate magnitude from several social indicators.

9

Integrating Need Information

Need analysis does not end with the identification of needs, but requires evaluation and integration of the need information for use in decision making. Evaluation of needs depends on the values underlying the analysis. Integration of multiple sources of need identification information is the major problem of need assessment. The use of multiattribute utility analysis for integration in needs assessment is presented in detail. The integration of information from multiple data sources is emphasized. Specific application is made to a need analysis for married university students.

Need analysis does not end with the assembly of a list of needs or problems and related supporting information. Need analysis requires evaluation and integration of information for use in decision making. This is the task of needs assessment. As discussed in Chapter 2, various needs assessment models emphasize different values. The decision-making model discussed in this chapter emphasizes the values of those who will act on the basis of the need analysis, the decision makers. The task of integrating the need identification information is common to all models of needs assessment, especially when multiple indicators are used. First, difficulties of information integration in need analysis are discussed, and then the application of decision analysis techniques (Pitz & McKillip, 1984) to solving these problems is presented in detail.

9.1 Problems of Information Integration in Need Analysis

Many critiques of need analysis have focused on the lack of a mechanism for meaningful integration of multiple indicators (e.g., *Health Service Program Needs Assessments Found Inadequate*, 1981; Kimmel, 1977). Two specific criticisms have been the reliance on rank orders of needs and the lack of attention to inconsistencies in results of different need identification methods.

Rank Order Is Not Enough!

Shapek (1975, p. 755) says:

One problem in assessing the significance of needs listings is related to the process of rank ordering. How important is one need compared to another?

Kimmel (1977) presents information contained in Table 9.1 taken from surveys of the citizens of Florida. Although community residents and human service system clients agree on four of the top five unmet needs in Florida, they disagree on the rank ordering. Key informants share only one need with the other groups (transportation). Kimmel (1977) asks: Where would you put your money if you were a Florida decision maker with $5 million to allocate? Table 9.1 does not help much in answering this question.

Multiple Decision Attributes

Decision makers can be consistent in their judgments when the information presented is simple. However, biases and inconsistencies appear when judgments require processing of complex multidimensional information (Kahneman et al., 1982).

Needs assessment models imply integration tasks of varying complexity (see Section 2.2). The task for the discrepancy model is the simplest since there is only one decision dimension. The discrepancy measure itself integrates information on performance expectations and actual outcomes (see Exhibits 2.1 and 6.1). The integration task for the marketing model is more difficult. Here, there are two decision dimensions: the attractiveness of the market and the cost of providing a service that will generate exchanges. When there are multiple options being considered, none may dominate (i.e., have the most attractive market *and* have the lowest cost of implementation). The integration task for the decision-making model is more difficult still, because the decision dimensions of performance expectancies, actual performance, solution cost, solution impact, and solution feasibility must be considered. No option is likely to be superior on all dimensions. The choice of one action over others requires tradeoffs among decision dimensions.

The task of integration becomes difficult for all needs assessment models as the number of sources of information used to identify needs increases (as recommended in Section 8.1). When there is more than one measure or attribute for each decision dimension, it is likely that tradeoffs will be required at this level. Part of the dissatisfaction with need analysis by program administrators and other decision makers

TABLE 9.1
Rank Order of Top Five Unmet Needs by Community, Clients, and Key Informants, State of Florida, Adapted from Kimmel, 1977

Community (N = 1187)	Clients (N = 1769)	Key Informants (N = 1154)
Routine dental care	Routine dental care	Unemployment
Food stamps	Financial assistance	Child abuse
Financial assistance	Food stamps	Malnutrition
Information and referral	Utility problems	Transportation
Transportation	Transportation	Low-income medical care

(*Health Service Program Needs Assessments Found Inadequate*, 1981) is due to the lack of guidance on how the tradeoffs required for the use of need analyses in decisions are to be made. Tradeoffs are made frequently by decision makers. Decision makers are not usually confronted with tradeoffs explicitly, however, as they are with a need analysis that reports conflicting indicators of multiple needs.

9.2 Multiattribute Utility Analysis, MAUA

This chapter presents a detailed example of the application of multiattribute utility analysis (MAUA) in needs assessment (see also Exhibit 2.3 in Section 2.2). The sample case is taken from Workman's (1980) need analysis for residents of a university's married student housing complex. First the case is introduced, then an overview of the MAUA procedure is presented. The next section applies MAUA to Workman's need identification. The final section of the chapter discusses assumptions of MAUA and extensions to other need analysis problems.

Married Student Housing
Need Identification

Workman (1980) conducted a need analysis[1] for the nearly 2000 residents of two married student housing complexes at a large midwestern state university. Residents in the complexes were university students, their spouses, and their children. Most students were married but a small number were single parents.

The analysis combined three sources of information, collected in response to a community forum of local human service providers.

(1) Telephone surveys were conducted with 118 randomly sampled residents of two housing complexes. As part of the survey, residents were asked to rate whether each of a series of ten sources of stress was a problem for their own families.

(2) Face-to-face interviews were conducted with 18 key informants. The key informants were asked to respond to the same ten sources of stress as the residents, judging whether they were a source of stress for the residents. The same response scale was used for both survey and interviews.

(3) A social indicator analysis was done based on university housing records, campus security records, and census data. Indicators of each problem were aggregated by an expert. These aggregated ratings were then standardized.

Scores for each of the 10 sources of stress studied are presented in Table 9.2. Results from the surveys of the two complexes were kept separate because they were meaningful locally. The task of needs assessment is to evaluate and synthesize the information in Table 9.2 to select sources of stress to be addressed by university personnel.

Overview of MAUA

Multiattribute utility analysis (MAUA) (Keeney & Raiffa, 1976; Pitz & McKillip, 1984) provides a prescriptive model of how decisions *ought* to be made, rather than of how they *are* made. Its principal technique is to break up a global judgment, have the decision maker make simpler judgments, and then mathematically integrate the simpler judgments into a global recommendation. In the sample case, the global judgment is the choice of problem areas to be addressed by new programming. The decision makers' task is to evaluate and synthesize the sometimes conflicting results of multiple need identification methods and to choose the "best" areas. Rather than require global judgments based on information such as Table 9.2, decision makers evaluate: (a) the relevance to the decision of the sources of information; and (b) the relationship between the scores that occur and need. MAUA then provides a mathematical rule for synthesizing these evaluations.

MAUA offers three advantages, besides requiring decision makers to make limited rather than global assessments. First, it utilizes the values of the decision maker(s) in the needs assessment instead of those of the

TABLE 9.2
Observed Attribute Scores from Married Student
Housing Need Identification Study

Potential Problems (Options)	Data Sources (Attributes)			
	Residents[a]			
	Complex A	Complex B	Key Informants[a]	Social Indicators[b]
Finances	2.12[c]	1.43	2.83	0.04
Unsupervised children	2.05	1.31	2.76	.76
Finding regular child care	1.43	1.13	2.82	1.12
Noise from outside apartment	1.76	1.37	2.33	0.04
Finding something to do	1.56	1.24	1.94	−0.69
People in apartment fighting	1.18	1.14	2.22	0.40
Transportation to university	1.30	1.33	1.94	−1.77
Crime	1.26	1.10	1.82	1.48
Finding a physician	1.15	1.20	1.88	−1.05
Lease with housing	1.27	1.12	1.29	−0.32

a. Average score ranging from 1 (not a problem) to 3 (a very important problem).
b. Standardized result from expert aggregation of multiple indicators.
c. Attribute scores.

researcher or some external body. Use of the decision maker's values increases the probability that the need analysis will be used to make decisions (Weiss & Bucuvalas, 1980). Second, the value judgments and tradeoffs supporting the global assessments are explicit. Third, MAUA provides a quantitative index of need that is comparable across the options being considered and reflects differences in magnitude as well as rank order.

MAUA proceeds in three stages: modeling, quantification, and synthesis. During the first stage, a model is constructed of the decision that is to be made. One component of the model is *options*, the choices confronting the decision maker. The rows of Table 9.2 present the options considered for the sample case. The other component of the models is *attributes*, the sources of information used for need identification. Attributes measure aspects of a problem or solution that the decision maker wants to consider. Attributes for the sample case are shown in the columns Table 9.2. Options and attributes are selected as a result of an iterative process like that presented in Section 1.1. As part of a need identification, each option receives a score on each attribute.

For the sample case, the attribute scores are the number presented in Table 9.2.

The quantification stage of MAUA provides techniques to evaluate attribute scores using the values of the decision maker. Attributes are transformed in two ways: attribute scores are rescaled as *utilities* to reflect how much need each indicates; and attributes themselves are given *weights* that reflect the relevance of the source of information for the decision. For example, in the sample case the decision maker evaluates the need indicated by a key informant rating of 2.83 (Finances) as compared to 2.22 (People in the Apartment Fighting) and the relevance of the key informants survey as a source of information.

The synthesis stage of MAUA integrates utilities and weights to compute a Need Index (N_i) for each option. This index has interval scale properties, revealing both order and magnitude of need. The additive integration rule is discussed. For other integration rules see Pitz and McKillip (1984).

Need identification results in a model for the decision and in attribute scores for each of the options under consideration. The modeling stage of MAUA is completed by a need identification. The quantification and synthesis stages constitute a needs assessment.

9.3 Application of MAUA

This section presents techniques for the quantification and the synthesis stages of MAUA. First, the steps are presented for developing utility functions that translate attributes scores to utility values. Next, a method is illustrated for weighting attributes. Finally, the additive integration rule is presented for synthesizing weights and utilities.

Quantification

Utility functions. The quantification stage of MAUA begins after need identification, with a matrix like Table 9.2. Utility functions are developed to translate the attribute scores in the cells of Table 9.2 into the utility values (n_{ij}s) in the cells of Table 9.3. Attribute scores are raw measurements. Utilities are the decision maker's evaluation of these scores as measures of need.[2] Utilities reflect preferences that the decision maker has for one score over another on an attribute as an indicator of need. A *utility function* is a rule for translating attribute scores into utility values. A separate utility function is developed for each attribute. For example, a utility function converts the score of 2.83 for the potential problem of Finances (row 1, Table 9.2) from the key informants interviews (column 3, Table 9.2) into the number .91 (row 1, column 3 of Table 9.3) that reflects the decision maker's evaluation of how much need the 2.83 indicates.

First, extreme utility values are assigned to high and low scores on each attribute. Utility values range from 0.0 to 1.0. A high utility value (close to 1.0) reflects an attribute score that the decision maker evaluates as indicating a great deal of need. A low utility value (close to 0.0) reflects a score that does not indicate a need to the decision maker. Although there is flexibility in assigning scores to extreme values, MAUA does not evaluate all possible attribute scores, but the range of scores that will be encountered in the particular analysis. If values are assigned before the observed range of scores is known, the lowest *probable* attribute score is assigned a utility of 0.0 and the highest probable score is assigned 1.0. If observed scores are known, scores equal to or just slightly more extreme than the highest and lowest observed scores should be used. For the resident and the key informant surveys in the married student housing example, utility of 0.0 was assigned to the attribute score of 1.1 and utility of 1.0 was assigned to the attribute score of 2.9. The observed range of scores was used for extreme utilities for the social indicators analysis, that is, utilities of 0.0 and 1.0 were to observed scores of -1.77 and 1.48, respectively.

The next step is the assignment of utilities to intermediate attribute scores. The simplest procedure is to assume a *linear* utility function, that utility increases or decreases equally with changes in the attribute scores. Utility values of intermediate scores is equal to:

$$n_{ij} = (X - L) / (H - L),$$

where n_{ij} is the utility value of option i on attribute j, X is the intermediate attribute score, L is the score of attribute j assigned the utility of 0.0, and H is the score of attribute j assigned 1.0

The assumption of a linear utility function was made for the residents' surveys and for the social indicator analysis. Need, indicated by higher attribute scores, was assumed to increase equally with increases in observed scores. For example, Complex A residents had a score of 2.12 on Finances as a problem. Using the extreme utility values discussed above, the observed score was transformed into a utility value by:

$$n_{1,1} = (2.12 - 1.1) \, / \, (2.9 - 1.1) = .57$$

Similarly the social indicator score of Finding a Physician was transformed into a utility value by:

$$n_{9,4} = (-1.05 - (-1.77)) \, / \, (1.48 - (-1.77)) = .20$$

In cases where changes over one part of the attribute scale are more important than changes over another part of the scale, a decision maker may be more comfortable with a logarithmic than a linear utility function. The enrollment attribute used in Exhibit 2.3 provides an example.

A second method of constructing a utility function is by *indifference judgments*. The condition under which a decision maker is indifferent between two outcomes on an attribute allows inferences about the utility function. In the example, the decision maker was unwilling to assume a linear utility function for key informants' responses, knowing that key informants tend to dramatize the seriousness of problems (Exhibit 6.2). Indifference judgments were used to quantify this utility function. Consider the following question concerning key informant scores:

Evidence for two potential problems is alike in all respects except that problem A has a key informant score of 1.1 and problem B has a key informant score of 2.0 (halfway between the extreme points of 1.1 and 2.9). Suppose that either problem A's score was increased to 2.0 or problem B's score was increased to 2.9. Which of these two increases would indicate the greatest need?

If the utility function were linear, the decision maker should consider both changes in attribute scores to reveal equal changes in need. If the decision maker does not, the utility function is probably nonlinear. The indifference question is modified to derive the point of indifference. For example, when the decision maker indicated that the change from 2.0 to 2.9 indicated greater need than from 1.1 to 2.0, this question was asked:

Evidence for two potential problems is alike in all respects except that problem A has a key informant score of 1.1 and problem B has a key informant score of 2.5. Suppose that either problem A's score was increased to 2.5 or problem B's score was increased to 2.9. Which of these two increases would indicate the greatest need?

The initial value assigned to problem B (e.g., 2.5) is adjusted until the decision maker is indifferent.

In the example, the decision maker was indifferent between a change of 1.1 to 2.75 and a change of 2.75 to 2.9. The implication is that the utility value of a key informant score of 2.75 is .50, halfway between the utilities of 0.0 and 1.0. Other intermediate utility values are now estimated (e.g., the attribute score for the utility value of .75, half way between observed values of 2.75 and 2.9). Once several utility values have been estimated, a utility function can be fit, by hand, to a graph similar to Figure 9.1.[3] Utility values can be read directly off such a graph. First, draw a perpendicular line from an attribute score on the x-axis to the utility function. Second, draw a perpendicular line from this point on the utility function to the y-axis. The value of point on the y-axis is the utility value for the attribute score on the x-axis.

Figure 9.1 shows utility functions for the resident and the key informant attributes of the need identification. The (linear) utility function for the resident surveys is shown by the diagonal line, equal increases in the attribute scores produce equal increases in utility values. The concave line is the utility function constructed by indifference judgments for key informant scores. Utility values increase more slowly than do attribute scores up to a point (2.75), and then increase more quickly than attribute scores. Once a utility function is constructed, intermediate values can be read off the graph. Utility values for the sample case are presented in Table 9.3.

Weights. The second part of the quantification stage of MAUA is development of a relevance weight for each attribute. The larger the weight, the more relevant the attribute is for the decision and the more important the attribute is in computing the Need Index (N_i). Weights are not general measures of importance. Weights reflect the decision maker's beliefs about how much attention should be paid to individual attributes in the context of the decision being made. The size of an attribute's weight is influenced *both* by the absolute difference in the attribute scores assigned extreme utilities (0.0 and 1.0) and by the relevance of the other attributes included in the needs assessment. An attribute's weight can be reduced to 0 if the range of observed scores is very small or if the number of relevant attributes is large. In Exhibit 2.3, because the cost of each continuing education course was about the same, the attribute of cost was so "unimportant" that it was not even included in the analysis!

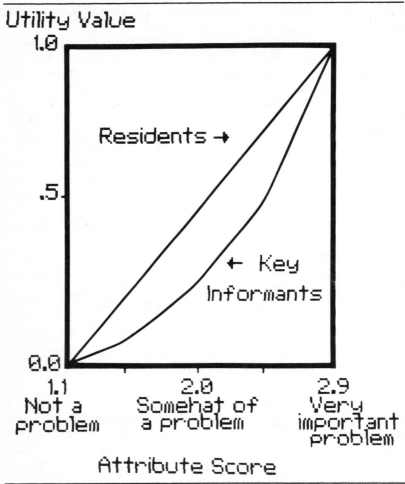

Figure 9.1   Utility Functions for Resident and Key Informant Survey Responses

Weights are assigned in three steps.[4] First, after considering the range of attributes scores assigned extreme utility values, attributes are ranked from most to least important. For our example, the attributes ordered by importance were residents, key informants, and social indicators.

Next, the most important attribute is assigned a weight of 100 and the decision maker is asked to assign a weight to the next most important

TABLE 9.3
Utility Values, Weights, and Need Index for
Married Student Housing Need Assessment Study

| | Data Sources (Attributes) | | | | |
| | Residents (.500)[a] | | | | |
Potential Problems (Options)	Complex A (.267)	Complex B (.233)	Key Informants (.333)	Social Indicators (.167)	Need Index (N_i)
Finances	.57[b]	.18	.91	.56	.59
Unsupervised children	.53	.12	.82	.78	.57
Finding regular child care	.18	.02	.90	.89	.50
Noise from outside apartment	.37	.15	.41	.56	.36
Finding something to do	.26	.08	.23	.33	.22
People in apartment fighting	.04	.02	.32	.67	.23
Transportation to university	.11	.13	.23	.00	.14
Crime	.09	.00	.20	1.00	.26
Finding a physician	.03	.06	.21	.22	.13
Lease with housing	.13	.06	.05	.04	.13

a. Weights, w_j. Weight for resident complexes was computed from the weight for the resident survey attribute according to the proportion of housing residents living in each complex.
b. Utilities, n_{ij}.

attribute. The weight reflects its relative importance. If this second attribute is assigned a 50, it is half as important as the top ranked attribute. If it is assigned a 25, it is only one quarter as important. In the example, residents' responses were assigned 100 and those of key informants were assigned a 66, indicating that key informants' responses were about two thirds as important as residents'. The third most important attribute is then compared to the top two attributes and assigned a weight. In the example, social indicators were assigned a weight of 34, half as important as key informant attribute and one-third as important as residents attribute. Use of multiple attributes allows for consistency checks on assigned weights and will occasionally cause reversals of importance rankings.

Finally, weights are standardized by adding all weights and dividing each weight by this sum:

$$\text{weight}_j = \frac{\text{Raw weight for attribute}}{\text{Sum of all importance weights}}$$

where weight $_j$ is the standardized weight for attribute j. Standardization guarantees that weights will vary from 0.0 to 1.0 and that the sum of weights will equal 1.

The weights for the example are shown in parentheses in Table 9.3. Complex A had more residents than complex B. The weight for the residents attribute was divided among the two complexes according to the proportion of residents in each complex. The quantification step of the MAUA is now complete. The first four columns of Table 9.3 reflect the decision maker's evaluation of the results of the need identification.

Synthesis

This stage integrates the results of the decision maker's evaluation. Utilities and weights are combined into the Need Index using an additive integration rule:

$$N_i = \Sigma \ (w_j * n_{ij}).$$

The Need Index for each option i, N_i, is equal to the sum over all attributes of the product of the weight of the attribute, w_j, and the utility of the attribute score for the option, n_{ij}. The Need Index ranges from 0.0, indicating no evidence of need (given the decision maker's values and the evidence available), to 1.0 indicating the maximum plausible evidence of need.

In the example, the Need Index for Finances is:

$$N_1 = .267* .57 + .233* .18 + .333* .91 + .167* .56 = .59$$

The Need Index values for the ten problems from the married student housing needs assessment are shown in the final column of Table 9.3. The Need Index integrates need identification information (e.g., Table 9.2) in a way that reflects the decision maker's values (n_{ij}s) and beliefs (w_js). The Need Index summarizes the needs assessment; it expresses the evaluation of the identified needs. How important is each? How does its importance compare to the other identified needs? The Need Index has interval properties so that both the rank order and the relative differences between index values have meaning. In the example, Finances is the top problem, followed closely by Unsupervised Children. The difference between these two is much smaller than that between Unsupervised Children and Finding Regular Child Care. The Need Index can be used to identify the most important needs and also to indicate how much more important one need is than another. The possibility of guidance for proportional allocation of resources is perhaps the most useful aspect of the index.

The quantification and synthesis stages of MAUA can be summarized in three steps:

(1) Translate attribute scores into utility values ($n_{ij}s$). Attributes are the data sources gathered for the need identification. Translation involves construction of utility functions. Where linear utility functions are not appropriate, monotonic functions can be developed.
(2) Assign weights ($w_j s$) to each attribute. The larger the weight, the more relevant the attribute is for the decision.
(3) Integrate the weight and utility values for each attribute using the additive integration rule to compute the Need Index.

9.4 Assumptions of MAUA and Extensions to Presentation

Attributes

The discussion of attributes assumed that all were measured so that higher scores indicated greater need than lower scores. MAUA will be easier if attribute scales are transformed to meet this assumption. A more important assumption about attributes was that they had monotonic utility functions: As attribute scores increased, utility values increased or stayed the same. Utility values did not increase and then decrease as attribute scores changed. Where this assumption is not true, transformation of attribute scales can make it true.

The most important assumption of MAUA is *preference independence*. If it does not hold, the additive integration rule cannot be used. Preference independence indicates that for any two attributes A and B, utility values for scores on one attribute, A, are independent of the score on the other attribute. If score A_1 has greater utility as an indicator of need than score A_2 when attribute B has the score B_1, then the ordering of A_1 and A_2 as indicators of need should be the same when attribute B has the score B_2. In our example, high resident survey scores (A_1) were taken as indicators of greater need than low survey scores (A_2) regardless of an option's score on the key informant's attribute (B). In need analysis, violations of the preference independence assumption are probably rare. In addition, problem attributes are less likely to violate preference independence than are solution attributes. Pitz and McKillip (1984) present tests for preference independence, and alternative integration rules for use when violations of the assumption cannot be mended.

Uncertainty

Probabilistic models of MAUA that explicitly incorporate risk or uncertainty have not been presented. It has been assumed that the attribute scores attached to an option were known. Sometimes uncertainty can be included as a separate attribute, for example, the "relevance of enrollment" attribute of Exhibit 2.3. Pitz and McKillip (1984) discuss other means for incorporating uncertainty into a MAUA.

Robustness

The Need Index values of Table 9.3 are dependent on the values of the decision maker and on the options and attributes included in the need identification. Different decision makers, different options, or different attributes would yield changed Need Index values. Thus MAUA results in an index that fits with the definition of need given in Chapter 1. Need is a judgment; need is dependent on the values of the judge. Some discussions of need analysis imply that judgmental, value-laden aspects of the process can be avoided. They cannot. MAUA makes the judgmental and value-laden aspects of analysis explicit and opens them to negotiation and experimentation.

MAUA does not necessarily end with the computation of the Need Index for possible problems. It should (as did Workman's study, 1980) include evidence about solutions. Solution-problem pairings can be used as options. Solutions also can be selected for identified problems by MAUA. Sensitivity analysis can be used to test whether the implications for action would differ if the Need Index were computed with different weights or utilities. Nagel (1985) and Pitz and McKillip (1984) discuss various forms of sensitivity analysis and their use for decision making.

MAUA can be considerably more flexible than the model presented in this section. Although need analysis usually uses quantitative measures, qualitative methods are increasingly popular (Chapter 7). For some attributes, such as the impact of solutions, subjective ratings may be the only indicator scale available. MAUA is not restricted to assessments that integrate only quantitative attributes. Finally, most need analyses are not conducted for a single decision maker. MAUA can be extended to include the values of multiple decision makers and audiences in a need assessment. Pitz and McKillip (1984) discuss these and other issues that affect the use of MAUA in applied research settings.

EXERCISES

1. Apply MAUA to the information contained in a published need analysis that included at least two sources of information and at least two options. Compare the recommendations of that study with the Need Index values you generate.
2. Compare the Need Index values you generate for Exercise 1 with those developed by someone else. Examine weights and utilities to identify sources of disagreement between the analyses.
3. Analyze the sensitivity of the weights and utilities you generated for Exercise 1. What changes in weights or utilities would cause a reversal of the order of Need Index values for the top two options for your analysis in Exercise 1. Which of these changes are reasonable? Which are not?

NOTES

1. Only the problem identification aspects of Workman's (1980) study are presented here.
2. In the version of MAUA considered here, utilities directly reflect the decision maker's values. Advanced applications of MAUA that include probabilistic models distinguish value functions from utility functions.
3. Utility functions can also be fit by a general linear polynomial of the form:

$$n = b_0 + b_1*X + b_2*X^2 + b_3*X^3 + \ldots$$

where b_0, b_1, ..., are estimated from utility values (Xs) already known.

4. Alternatives exist for this and other procedures discussed in this section (Pitz & McKillip, 1984).

10

Communication of Results

Communication of the results of a need analysis is critical if the analysis is to affect decisions. Techniques for written, graphic, and oral presentation of need analysis findings are reviewed. The content of research reports and executive summaries is presented. Detailed recommendations are given for the construction and use of tables and graphs. A procedure for oral briefings is presented.

Communication between decision makers and researchers is important at every phase of a need analysis. Decisions about the scope of the analysis, about when to start and when to stop gathering information, and about what data-gathering methods to use should only be reached after consultation and consideration of alternatives (Section 8.2).

Communication of the results of the analysis is even more important because it will determine if and how the analysis will affect decisions. Communications must be fit to audience interests. The audience for need analysis reports is similar to that for other applied research: they are usually busy and are often unsophisticated about research. Lay members of boards of directors will be particularly rejecting of lengthy and technically or professionally-oriented manuscripts. Reports should be designed not as archives for evidence of the writer's statistical sophistication but to attract the interest and provoke the understanding of the readers. Technical information on such issues as sample selection and interviewer training can be recorded separately, in appendices or separate reports, following the disciplinary format of the writer.

This chapter reviews means of attracting and provoking potential users of need analysis reports through written, graphic, and oral presentation of findings.

10.1 Written Communications

Written need analysis reports should be characterized by attractive layout, clarity of language, and interest value of content. Reports should be bound and use thick paper covers. The cover should show the report title, its authors, and the logo of their agency or organization. Colored page breaks between sections of the report increase its use as a reference document.

The language of reports should be as free of technical terms as possible. Readability analysis is helpful (Section 6.2). Correct spelling, grammar, and sentence structure are prerequisites of report credibility.

Reports are written to encourage and to respond to the interests of those who read them. Reports should cover the topics of interest to the audience, given the decisions to be made, as well as provide information to support evaluation of these topics. Any broad research effort will gather more information than eventually is required for decisions. If information is not needed by the audience, it should not be in the report. Depending on the divergent interests of the audiences for the need analysis, more than one report may be required.

Report Organization

A need analysis report will generally have four sections:

- Executive summary
- Scope, and methods used
- Results of study
- Implications

Applied research reports start with an *executive summary*. A good summary can spur the interest of potential readers. It provides information for those without the time (or inclination) to read the full report, and for those whose interests are served by a quick overview (e.g., for an agency's newsletter). Stalford (1985) has these suggestions for executive summaries:

(1) Keep them short, 1½-4 pages.
(2) Use plain language, *no* jargon here.
(3) Simplify findings. Present the main points ignoring qualifying interactions.
(4) Include qualitative judgments of implications. Quantitative information and cautions belong in the report itself.

Macy (1982) has two other useful suggestions for summarizing information: memos and embedded quotations. Memos differ from executive summaries because they are not attached to a report. Memos are free to find interested parties whereas thicker reports might scare off the wary. Embedded quotations are abridged or direct quotations from the text of a report that are highlighted within the body of the report. They serve to catch the eye of potential readers as they page through the report. Taken together, embedded quotations can provide a summary of the report.

The *scope and method section* lists the questions that are addressed in the report as well as the data-gathering techniques used. Usually a short description of the methods is all that is necessary. Intricacies of their application are best left to a technical appendix or to a separate report. Aspects of the methodology that severely limit a report's credibility should be mentioned, with detail presented in a technical appendix or report.

The *results section* of the report should first summarize the results. Findings for the target population should then be presented along with comparable information (expectancies) that allows readers to evaluate these results. Organization of the section should maximize ease of comparison. For example, paging back and forth between presentations of actual and expected outcomes of the target population should be minimized. It may be necessary to repeat information to facilitate comparison. Use of tables and graphs facilitate comparisons and understanding. Qualitative information, such as anecdotes of inter- viewers or specific quotations from open-ended questions, is also crucial to the reader's understanding and appreciation of the study. Numbers are not enough! The thoughts and comments of clients, key informants, and others involved will help the reader visualize, evaluate, and accept a quantitative message.

It is important that a report make explicit the *implications* of the analysis for action, if only for the reader to consider and reject recommendations. For credibility, the implications and the results sections should be separated.

10.2 Tables

The microcomputer revolution has brought graphics capability to almost any report writer. However, like any tool, the computer must be directed to produce anything of value. Happily, theoretical and practical guidance is available for the appropriate use of tabular and graphic presentations (Ehrenberg, 1977; Schmid, 1983; Tufte, 1983; Wainer, 1984). This section presents recommendations for the use of tables. The next section presents recommendations and examples of the use of graphs.

According to Tufte (1983), text should be used to present two numbers, tables to present 3-20 numbers, and graphs more than 20 numbers. Tables are particularly powerful for making comparison along a column of numbers and do not require the reorientation from textual material that accompany graphs. Most of us have been presented with too many poorly done tables to believe Tufte's recommendation. Ehrenberg (1977) gives five rules that allow tables to realize their potential as communication devices:

(1) Round numbers to two significant or effective digits. Significant digits are those that vary in the data.
(2) Include row and column average in the table.
(3) Put the numbers that are most important to compare in columns rather than rows.
(4) Order rows and columns by size, rather than, for example, alphabetically or geographically.
(5) Space rows that need to be compared close together.

Tables 10.1 and 10.2 present an example of the applications of these principles.

10.3 Graphs and Figures

Interesting graphics reflect interesting data, or as Denis Johnston[1] says: "A good graph deserves 1000 words." Graphs are powerful means of communication and should be reserved for those relationships that are worthy of lengthy discussion. Simple relationships can easily be displayed and understood in tabular form. Graphs are best for showing relationships between two or more measures or classifications. This section discusses rules for developing graphs, and presents and discusses examples of bar and column graphs and maps. Detailed presentation of these issues can be found in Schmid (1983) and Tufte (1983).

Rules for Graph Design

In need analysis, graphs are meant to communicate information about relationships, especially where intense inspection will deepen a

TABLE 10.1
Example of Poor Table Construction,
Abortion Ratios[a] by Age and Race, 1979

	14 & under	15-19	20-24	25-29	30-34	35-39	40 & over
White	1634.6	809.3	363.6	194.5	209.0	382.8	806.4
Black	1218.8	559.7	600.3	567.0	594.2	804.7	1169.8

a. Number of abortions per 100 live births, National Center for Health Statistics.

TABLE 10.2
Example of Improved Table Construction,
Abortion Ratios by Age and Race, 1979

Age	Total	White	Black
14 & under	1400	1600	1200
15-19	730	810	560
20-24	410	370	600
25-29	250	190	570
30-34	260	210	590
35-39	460	380	805
40 & over	880	810	1200
Total	390	340	600

NOTE: Number of abortions per 100 live births, National Center for Health Statistics.

reader's understanding of the relationship. Graphs are an outgrowth of the use of maps. The essential task in the development of a graph is to replace latitude and longitude (length and height) with measures not based on the geographic analogy. The first principle of graph design, as given by Tufte (1983) is that *design variation should reflect data variation* alone, and nothing else. Differences that occur in the data should be reflected in differences in the graph. Embellishments and redundancies do not serve accurate communication and confuse and distract the reader. Wainer (1984) presents examples. This principle implies the following:

(1) Because numbers vary in both order (one is larger than the other) and magnitude (differences between numbers can be compared), both characteristics should be reflected accurately in the graph.
   • Length and height can directly reflect differences in order and magnitude.

- Area (e.g., circles) and volume (e.g., cylinders) pose problems for graphic presentation because they increase exponentially with changes in length or height and distort presentation of changes along a single dimension. Use of three dimensional graphics complicates the reader's task, unless the third dimension reflects meaningful variation in the data.
- Thin bars or columns better reflect variation along a single dimension than do thick bars or columns.
- Color, except shades of gray, is not useful for showing quantitative variation along a single dimension. Color changes reflect multidimensional rather than unidimensional differences.

(2) Visual aspects of the chart that do not reflect data variation are not needed.

- Moire vibrations distract the reader from the graph. Visual wavelike effects are maximized by equally spaced lines. The cross-hatching that so characterizes microcomputer graphic programs should be replaced by shades of gray. For graphs that will be photographed with high contrast film, stipple patterns of shading film should replace crosshatching or regular dot patterns.
- Baselines can be used to carry information about the range and distribution of variations.

(3) The most egregious inaccuracies in graphing come from lack of attention to baseline variation.

- Changes in baseline should stand out to the reader and reflect important variations in the data. Intervals that appear equal on the graph should reflect equal-sized intervals in the data.
- Breaks in baseline should be clear. Schmid (1983) recommends that baselines routinely start at zero.
- Data should be adjusted for subtle changes in baseline before graphing. Monetary values should be adjusted for inflation and incidence and prevalence estimates should be adjusted for changes in population size.

A second principle of graphic design is to *keep graphics friendly* (Tufte, 1983).

(1) The same lettering, upper and lower case, used in the text should be used on the graphics. Crude plotter lettering is discouraged.

(2) Labels should be simple but informative on their own. Abbreviations are discouraged. Labels should be typed horizontally, not vertically. The reader should be able to make sense out of a graph without reference to the text.

(3) Because of our sensitivity to slight visual changes, graphs can contain a good deal of information. Lots of white space and limitation to a few data points are unnecessary. Graphs can be reduced to allow multiple presentations on a single page where comparison between graphs is important, for example, Figure 10.1.

(4) A ratio of length to height of 1.5:1 is recommended.

Bar, Column, and Pie Graphs

Bar and column graphs are useful for showing the relationship between dichotomous variables and outcome measures, bars running vertically and columns horizontally. Because comparisons down a column are easier to make than across a row and because vertical labels are easier to read than horizontal labels, bar graphs are better than column graphs. Where comparison of multiple trends is required, line graphs are better than column graphs. Because perception of area, especially of circles, is uneven and comparison between areas is difficult, pie graphs have little to recommend them.

Figures 10.1 and 10.2 present a series of bar and column graphs. Schmid (1983), *Social Indicators 1976* (1977) and *Social Indicators III* (1980) provide other (good and bad) examples of bar and column graphs.[2]

The *Simple Bar Graph* does not usually offer advantages over tabular presentation. As in tables, classifications should be ordered by size, not alphabetically or geographically. One or two subdivisions within bars are possible, more than two presents the reader with a difficult comparative task.

The *Paired Bar Graph*, perhaps most frequently seen as an age (vertical presentation) -sex (horizontal panels) pyramid. This graph allows easy comparison of two related measures.

The *Deviation Bar Graph* permits comparison of outcomes with some standard (e.g., above or below poverty level, profit, or loss). The *Sliding Bar Graph* facilitates comparisons of magnitudes on a single question (e.g., percentage satisfied versus percentage dissatisfied). The length of the bar reflects the total of the two categories. Both graphs present alternatives to a subdivided bar graph.

The *Range Graph* (Schmid, 1983) provides an example of how simplification can increase information and aid understanding. In the revised graph small squares show median values and lines show the distances from the first or third quartiles to the minimum and maximum values, respectively. The revised range graph adds two additional pieces

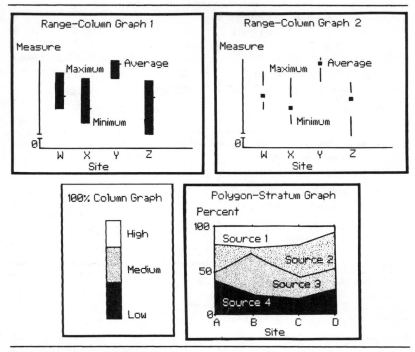

Figure 10.1 Examples of Bar Graphs

of information for each classification period while being simpler to look at.

The *100% Column Graph* presents an alternative to the Pie Graph. The *Stratum-Polygon Graph* illustrates a comparison that would be nearly impossible if done through a series of Pie Graphs. The length dimension (x-axis) can be either nominal or ordinal. Comparisons are also easier than with a series of 100% column graphs.

Line graphs

Line graphs are useful for showing the relationship between continuous variables and outcome variables, especially change over time. In an x,y coordinate system, the x-axis, or abscissa, is usually used to array a causal or predictor variable and the y-axis, or ordinate, dislays the effect or criterion variable. Multiple trend lines may be included on a

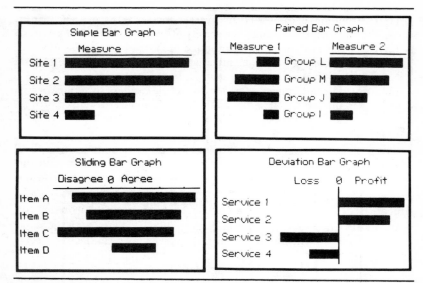

Figure 10.2   Examples of Column and Line Graphs

single graph. Trend lines can be drawn for separate subgroups of a target population or to display the interaction of one predictor variable with another. Transformations of outcome measures sometimes can lessen the number of lines needed to be included on a graph. Outcomes can be expressed

- as a percentage of a standard, such as of the outcomes of the best performing unit.
- as a ratio of a comparison group's outcome, for example, female/male unemployment.
- as an indexed number, such as the Consumer Price Index.

Wang (1978) presents ideas for display of multivariate data that may be of use for need analysis.

Maps

Maps provide a flexible and interesting format for presenting and analyzing geographically organized data (Monk & Hastings, 1981). Smith (1982) discusses three uses for maps:

(1) Distributions of cases or clients over the area served by an agency can be shown. Such maps display the density of events, problems, or services.

(2) Computer analysis of the distribution of cases can produce surface or contour maps and allow multivariate analyses of importance of geographic variables.

(3) Most frequently, maps are used to display the results of social area or risk factor analyses (Sections 4.2 and 4.3). Geographic areas are colored or shaded to reflect the intensity of problems, or the density of services.

Three problems occur with the most frequent uses of maps in applied research. First, the reader may confuse the geographical area with the seriousness of a problem. For example, on a map showing the average educational level in a region, a large, sparsely settled area with low educational attainment might appear to be a greater problem (or opportunity) than a smaller, but more densely settled area with the same level of educational attainment. The larger area may be taken to reflect a greater problem, when, in terms of number of people, the opposite is the case. Second, the impression is given that problems or solutions are evenly spread throughout an area. In an urban setting, an area as small as a census tract (Section 4.4) may contain wide variations in social class or other important variables. Such differences are lost when the average value is shown for the area. Third, geographic boundaries, shaded to reflect average values, give the impression of abrupt changes in status, when changes actually may be gradual.

Schmid (1983) reviews solutions to the problems of the use of maps. Most center on an alternative geometric shape that is imposed on each geographical area. These symbols, often circles or spheres, are shaded or enlarged to indicate quantitative values. Problems with the perception of area remain.

10.4 Oral Presentations

Hendricks (1982) gives an overview of a practical oral briefing procedure developed to report applied research findings to the top administrators of the U.S. Department of Health and Human Services. The briefings reported evaluations modeled after investigative reporting, combining review of documentation, interviews with participants, and observation. The advantages of oral briefings are that they combine personal contact with the exchange of information and that they allow a specific time for otherwise busy users of applied research to concentrate on the findings of a study.

The key to oral briefings is the speaker. Only a single presenter is used. The credibility of the presentation depends on the speaker's fluency with the research study and its findings. Fluency comes with practice and study of the research materials.

Hendricks (1982) suggests that an agenda and a report on the study be circulated ahead of the briefing, that the briefing itself be planned to take only one-third of the time scheduled, and that considerable attention be paid to audiovisual components of the presentation. Large charts are displayed throughout the briefing, summarizing the methods and findings of the study. Slides, overheads, and audiotapes are used to give the audience a qualitative feel for the topic of the briefing: Who make up the target population? What is their status? Where do they live? What services are available now?

Conduct of a briefing follows this schedule:

- introduction of the speaker by someone of equal status to the audience,
- summary of the issues to be covered in the briefing,
- brief description of the methods used in the study,
- audiovideo presentation on the people and services studied,
- presentation of results of the study,
- presentation of comparison information useful in evaluating the results, and
- interpretation of the findings

After the presentation the speaker and other support staff from the research project answer questions raised by the audience. Assignment of follow-up tasks arising out of the discussion is done during the session itself. The procedure is easily adapted to the presentation of the results of a need analysis to a policy making board or to other action-oriented audiences.

EXERCISES

1. Prepare an executive summary for a published need analysis report. What information is missing from the report?

2. Critique the tables and graphs used in a published need analysis report. Redesign the tables and graphs in line with the recommendations of this chapter.

3. Develop a map of your county or city, shading areas to reflect the

proportion of population that is overweight (Chapter 4, Exercise 2). How do the criticisms of maps made in the chapter apply to your work?

NOTES

1. Editor of several graphic presentations of federal statistics, including *Social Indicators 1976* and *Social Indicators III*.

2. Schmid's (1983) recommendation that background grids be used in most graphs is not followed here.

REFERENCES

Abraham, S., & Johnson, C. L. (1979). Overweight adults in the United States. *Advancedata, 51,* 1-11.

American Statistical Index. Bethesda, MD: Congressional Information Services.

Bachrach, K. M., & Zautra, A. (1980). Some uses of client and census records in community mental health planning. *American Journal of Community Psychology, 8,* 365-378.

Bernstein, P. W. (1978, January). Psychographics is still an issue on Madison Avenue. *Fortune,* pp. 78-84.

Bradshaw, J. (1972). The concept of social need. *New Society, 30,* 640-643.

Broskowski, A. (1983). The application of general systems theory in the assessment of community needs. In R. A. Bell, M. Sundel, J. F. Aponte, S. A. Murrell, & E. Lin (Eds.), *Assessing health and human service needs* (pp. 71-87). New York: Human Sciences Press.

Cagle, L. T. (1984). Using social indicators to assess mental health needs: Lessons from a statewide study. *Evaluation Review, 8,* 389-412.

Calder, B. J. (1977). Focus groups and the nature of qualitative marketing research. *Journal of Marketing Research, 14,* 353-364.

Campbell, D. T., & Fiske, D. W. (1959). Convergent and discriminant validation by the multitrait-multimethod matrix. *Psychological Bulletin, 56,* 81-105.

Carter, D. E., & Newman, F. L. (1976). A *client-oriented system of mental health service delivery and program management* (017-024-00523-1). Washington, DC: Superintendent of Public Documents.

Ciarlo, J. A., & Shern, D. L. (1985). *Validity models for estimating mental health-related need.* Paper presented at Evaluation '85, Toronto, Canada.

CIS Annual. Bethesda, MD: Congressional Information Services.

Cook, T. D., & Campbell, D. T. (1979). *Quasi-experimentation: Design and analysis of issues for field settings.* Chicago: Rand McNally.

Cox, C. C., Higginbotham, J. B., & Burton, J. (1976). Applications of focus groups interviews in marketing. *Journal of Marketing, 40,* 77-80.

Crano, W. D. (1981). Triangulation and cross-cultural research. In M. B. Brewer & B. E. Collins (Eds.), *Scientific inquiry and the social sciences* (pp. 317-344). San Francisco: Jossey-Bass.

Cummings, O. W. (1984). *Comparison of three algorithms for analyzing questionnaire type needs assessment data to establish needs priorities.* Paper presented at Evaluation '84, San Francisco.

Cummings, O. W., & Bramlett, M. H. (1984). *Needs assessment: A maximizing strategy that works for information development.* Paper presented at Evaluation '84, San Francisco.

Datta, L. (1978). Front-end analysis: Pegasus or shank's mare. *New Directions for Program Evaluation, 1,* 13-30.

Deaux, E., & Callaghan, J. W. (1984). Estimating statewide health-risk behavior: A comparison of telephone and key informant survey approaches. *Evaluation Review, 8*, 467-492.

Deaux, E., & Callaghan, J. W. (1985). Key informant versus self-report estimates of health-risk behavior. *Evaluation Review, 9*, 365-368.

Delbecq, A. L. (1983). The nominal group as a technique for understanding the qualitative dimensions of client needs. In R. A. Bell, M. Sundel, J. F. Aponte, S. A. Murrell, & E. Lin (Eds.), *Assessing health and human service needs* (pp. 210-218). New York: Human Sciences Press.

Dillman, D. (1978). *Mail and telephone surveys: The total design method*. New York: John Wiley.

Dohrenwend, B. P., Dohrenwend, B. S., Gould, M. S., Link, B., Neugebauer, R., & Wunsch-Hitzig, R. (1980). *Mental illness in the United States*. New York: Praeger.

Dunhan, H. W. (1983). The epidemiologic study of mental illness: Its value for needs assessment. In R. A. Bell, M. Sundel, J. F. Aponte, S. A. Murrell, & E. Lin (Eds.), *Assessing health and human service needs* (pp. 40-52). New York: Human Sciences Press.

Eaton, W. W. (1980). Demographic and social-ecological risk factors for mental disorders. In D. A. Regier & G. Allen (Eds.), *Risk factor research in the major mental disorders* (DHHS Publication No. ADM 81-1068). Washington, DC: Superintendent of Public Documents.

Eaton, W. W., Regier, D. A., Locke, B. Z., & Taube, C. A. (1981). The epidemiologic catchment area program of the National Institute of Mental Health. *Public Health Reports, 96*, 319-325.

Edwards, W., & Newman, J. R. (1982). *Multiattribute evaluation*. Newbury Park, CA: Sage.

Ehrenberg, A.S.C. (1977). Rudiments of numeracy. *Journal of the Royal Statistical Society, 140*, Series A, 277-297.

Ellsworth, R. B. (1979). Does follow-up reflect poor outcomes? *Evaluation in the Health Professions, 2*, 418-437.

Federal Depository Library Program (0-417-647 QL3). (1983). Washington, DC: Superintendent of Public Documents.

Filstead, W. J. (1979). Qualitative methods. In C. Reichardt & T. D. Cook (Eds.), *Qualitative and quantitative methods in evaluation research* (pp. 33-48). Newbury Park, CA: Sage.

Fitzgerald, C. T., & Cutler, W. (1983). *Resource inventory and directory of services for Jackson County, Illinois*. Carbondale: Southern Illinois University, Applied Research Consultants.

Flesch, R. (1960). *How to write, speak, and think more effectively*. New York: Harper & Row.

Flores, T. R. (1975). Student personnel programs for married students: A needs assessment. *Journal of College Student Personnel, 16*, 154-159.

Fowler, F. J. (1984). *Survey research methods*. Newbury Park, CA: Sage.

Frank, R. G. (1983). Is there a shortage of psychiatrists? An economist's view of the evidence. *Community Mental Health Journal, 19*, 42-53.

Goldsmith, H. F., Jackson, D. J., Doenhoefer, S., Johnson, W., Tweed, D. L., Stiles, D., Barbano, J. D., & Warheit, G. (1984). *The health demographic profile system's inventory of small area social indicators* (1984-455-749/20133). Washington, DC: Superintendent of Public Documents.

Goldsmith, H. F., Unger, E., Windle, C. D., Shambaugh, J. P., & Rosen, B. M. (1981). *A typological approach to doing social area analysis* (1981-341-166/6337). Washington, DC: Superintendent of Public Documents.

Guba, E. G. (1981). Criteria for assessing the trustworthiness of naturalistic inquiries. *ECTJ, 29*, 75-91.

Hagedorn, H. J. (1977). *A manual on state mental health planning* (017-024-00649-1). Washington, DC: Superintendent of Public Documents.

Hagedorn, H. J., Beck, K. J., Neubert, S. F., & Werlin, S. F. (1976). *A working manual of simple program evaluation techniques for community mental health centers* (DHEW Publication No. ADM 76-4041). Washington, DC: Superintendent of Public Documents.

Health service program needs assessments found inadequate (1981 341-843/682). (1981). Washington, DC: Superintendent of Public Documents.

Hendricks, M. (1982). Oral policy briefings. In N. L. Smith (Ed.), *Communication strategies in evaluation* (pp. 249-258). Newbury Park, CA: Sage.

Holsti, O. R. (1969). *Content analysis for the social sciences and humanities*. Reading, MA: Addison-Wesley.

Holzer, C. E., Jackson, D. J., & Tweed, D. (1981). Horizontal synthetic estimation. *Evaluation and Program Planning, 4*, 29-34.

Holzer, C. E., & Robins, L. (1981). Measurement issues in mental health needs assessment. In D. J. Jackson & E. F. Borgatta (Eds.), *Factor analysis and measurement in sociological research* (pp. 149-176). Newbury Park, CA: Sage.

Joint Commission on Accreditation of Hospitals. (1979). *Principles for accreditation of community mental health service programs*. Chicago: Author.

Kahneman, D., Slovic, P., & Tversky, A. (Eds.). (1982). *Judgment under uncertainty: Heuristics and biases*. Cambridge: Cambridge University Press.

Kaplan, C. P., & Van Valey, T. L. (1980). *Census 80: Continuing the fact finding tradition* (003-024-02262-1). Washington, DC: Superintendent of Public Documents.

Kauffman, R., & English, F. W. (1979). *Needs assessment concepts and application*. Englewood Cliffs, NJ: Educational Technology Publications.

Keeney, R. L., & Raiffa, H. (1976). *Decisions with multiple objectives: Preferences and value tradeoffs*. New York: John Wiley.

Kimmel, W. (1977). *Needs assessment: A critical perspective*. Washington, DC: Department of Health, Education and Welfare, Office of Program Systems.

Kotler, P. (1982). *Marketing for nonprofit organizations* (2nd ed.). Englewood Cliffs, NJ: Prentice-Hall.

Larsen, D., Attkisson, C., Hargreaves, W., & Nguyen, T. (1979). Assessment of client/patient satisfaction: Development of general scale. *Evaluation and Program Planning, 2*, 197-207.

Lauffer, A. (1982). *Assessment tools for practitioners, managers and trainers*. Newbury Park, CA: Sage.

Lavrakas, P. (1987). *Telephone survey methods: Sampling, selection, and supervision*. Newbury Park, CA: Sage.

Lebow, J. (1982). Consumer satisfaction with mental health treatment. *Psychological Bulletin, 91*, 244-259.

Levin, H. (1983). *Cost-effectiveness: A primer*. Newbury Park, CA: Sage.

Link, B., & Dohrenwend, B. P. (1980). Formulation of hypotheses about the ratio of

Link, B., & Dohrenwend, B. P. (1980). Formulation of hypotheses about the ratio of untreated to treated cases in true prevalence studies of functional psychiatric disorders in adults in the United States. In B. P. Dohrenwend et al., *Mental illness in the United States* (pp. 133-149). New York: Praeger.

Linstrom, H. A., & Turoff, M. (Eds.). (1975). *The Delphi method*. Reading, MA: Addison-Wesley.

Lobb, J., Young, L., & Ciarlo, J. A. (1979). Predicting relative utilization of community mental health facilities in the city and county of Denver. In G. Landsberg, W D. Neigher, R. J. Hammer, C. Windle, & J. R. Woy, *Evaluation in practice* (1980 0-318-017) (pp. 32-33). Washington, DC: Superintendent of Public Documents.

Lockhart, D. C. (1984). *Making effective use of mailed questionnaires*. San Francisco: Jossey-Bass.

Long, J. S. (1983). *An evaluation of the focused group interview as an adult education needs assessment technique*. Paper presented at Evaluation '83, Chicago.

Longest, J., Konan, M., & Tweed, D. (1979). *A study of the deficiencies and differentials in the distribution of mental health resources and facilities* (017-024-00962-8). Washington, DC: Superintendent of Public Documents.

Macy, D. J. (1982). Research briefs. In N. L. Smith (Ed.), *Communication strategies in evaluation* (pp. 179-189). Newbury Park, CA: Sage.

Marti-Costa, S., & Serrono-Garcia, I. (1983). Needs assessment and community development: An ideological perspective. *Prevention in Human Services, 3*, 75-83.

McKillip, J., & Kulp, J. (1985). College students' interest in sex go farther than STDS and contraception. *Health , 9*, 13-16.

Milcarek, B. I., & Link, B. G. (1981). Handling problems of ecological fallacy in program planning and evaluation. *Evaluation and Program Planning, 4*, 23-28.

Misanchuk, E. R. (1984). Analysis of multi-component educational and training needs. *Journal of Instructional Development, 7*, 28-33.

Monk, J. J., & Hasting, J. T. (1981). Geography. In N. L. Smith (Ed.), *Metaphors for evaluation: Sources of new methods* (pp. 137-180). Newbury Park, CA: Sage.

Monthly Catalogue of U.S. Government Publications. Washington, DC: Superintendent of Public Documents.

Moore, C. M. (1987). *Group techniques to generate, develop, and select ideas*. Newbury Park, CA: Sage.

Nagel, S. S. (1985). New varieties of sensitivity analysis. *Evaluation Review, 9*, 772-779.

Newbould, G. D. (1980, Spring). Product portfolio diagnosis for U.S. universities. *Akron Business and Economic Review*, pp. 39-45.

Newman, F. L., & Rinkus, A. (1978). Level of functioning, clinical judgment and mental health service evaluation. *Evaluation and the Health Professions, 1*, 175-194.

Nickerns, J. M., Purga, A. J., & Noriega, P. P. (1980). *Research methods for needs assessment*. Washington, DC: University Press of America.

Patton, M. Q. (1980). *Qualitative evaluation methods*. Newbury Park, CA: Sage.

Petersen, V. J., Bosanac, E. M., Baranowski, T., & Forren, G. L. (1981). *A resource inventory approach to needs assessment: Examples from a statewide hypertension control program*. Morgantown, WV: Department of Community Medicine, Office of Health Service Research.

Piasecki, J. R., & Kamis-Gould, E. (1981). Social area analysis in program evaluation and planning. *Evaluation and Program Planning, 4*, 3-14.

Pitz, G. F., & McKillip, J. (1984). *Decision analysis for program evaluators.* Newbury Park, Ca: Sage.

Posavac, E. J., & Carey, R. G. (1985). *Program evaluation methods and case studies* (2nd ed.). Englewood Cliffs, NJ: Prentice-Hall.

Regier, D. A., Goldberg, I. D., Kessler, L. G., & Burns, B. J. (1980). Overview of the three reports covering four health care settings. In I. D. Goldberg, D. A. Regier, & B. J. Burns (Eds.), *Use of health and mental health outpatient services in four organized health care settings* (1980 0 330130). Washington, DC: Superintendent of Public Documents.

Regier, D. A., Meyers, J. K., Kramer, M., Robins, L. N., Blazer, D. G., Hough, R. L., Eaton, W. W., & Locke, B. Z. (1984). The NIMH epidemiologic catchment area program. *Archives of General Psychiatry, 41,* 934-941.

Roitman, D. B. (1981). *Identifying community energy conservation programming needs with qualitative needs assessment approaches.* Paper presented at the Third National Conference on Needs Assessment, Louisville, KY.

Rosen, B. M., & Goldsmith, H. F. (1981). The health demographic profile system. *Evaluation and Program Planning, 4,* 57-73.

Rosenstein, M. J., & Bass, R. D. (1979). *The characteristics of persons served by the federally funded community mental health centers program, 1974* (DHEW Pub. No. ADM 79-771). Washington, DC: Superintendent of Public Documents.

Rosenstein, M. J., & Milazzo-Sayre, L. J. (1981). *Characteristics of admission to selected mental health facilities, 1975* (DHHS Publication No. ADM 81-1005). Washington, DC: Superintendent of Public Documents.

St. John, M. (1984). Committees: Their use in evaluation. In P. J. Gray & J. F. Turnidge (Eds.), *Guides to evaluation methods* (pp. 135-146). Portland, OR: Northwest Regional Educational Laboratory.

Schmid, C. F. (1983). *Statistical graphics, design principals and practices.* New York: John Wiley.

Schwab, J. J. (1983). Identifying and assessing needs: A synergism of social forces. In R. A. Bell, M. Sundel, J. F. Aponte, S. A. Murrell, & E. Lin (Eds.), *Assessing health and human service needs* (pp. 31-39). New York: Human Sciences Press.

Scriven, M., & Roth, J. (1978). Needs assessment: Concept and practice. *New Directions for Program Evaluation, 1,* 1-11.

Shapek, R. A. (1975, December). Problems and deficiencies in the needs assessment process. *Public Administration Review,* pp. 754-758.

Siegel, L. M., Attkisson, C. C., & Carson, L. G. (1978). Need identification and program planning in the community context. In C. C. Attkisson, W. A. Hargreaves, M. J. Horwitz, & J. E. Sorensen (Eds.), *Evaluation of human service programs* (pp. 215-252). New York: Academic Press.

Smith, Jana K., Falvo, D., McKillip, J., & Pitz, G. F. (1984). Measuring patient perceptions of the patient doctor interaction: Development of the PDIS. *Evaluation in the Health Professions, 7,* 77-94.

Smith, John K. (1983 March). Quantitative versus qualitative research: An attempt to qualify the issues. *Educational Researcher,* pp. 6-13.

Smith, N. L. (1982). Geographic displays. In N. L. Smith (Ed.), *Communication strategies in evaluation* (pp. 233-248). Newbury Park, CA: Sage.

Social Indicators 1976 (041-0010156-5). (1977). Washington, DC: Superintendent of Public Documents.

Social Indicators III (1980-0-328-848). (1980). Washington, DC: Superintendent of Public Documents.

Sorensen, J. L., Hammer, R., & Windle, C. (1979). The four A's—acceptability, availability, accessibility, awareness: Overview. In G. Landsberg, W. D. Neigher, R. J. Hammer, C. Windle, & J. R. Woy, *Evaluation in practice* (1980 0-318-017) (pp. 69-75).

Stalford, C. B. (1985). Reflections on writing a clear executive summary. *Evaluation News, 6*, 10-16.

Steadham, S. V. (1980, January). Learning to select a needs assessment strategy. *Training and Development Journal*, pp. 56-61.

Stengel, N. (1982). Commitee hearings. In N. L. Smith (Ed.), *Communication strategies in evaluation* (pp. 279-288). Newbury Park, CA: Sage.

Sudman, S. S., & Bradburn, N. M. (1982). *Asking questions*. San Francisco: Jossey-Bass.

Sumariwalla, R. D. (1976). *UWASIS II: A taxonomy of social goals and human service programs*. Alexandria, VA: United Way of America.

Taube, C., Lee, E. S., & Forthofer, R. N. (1984). Diagnosis-related groups for mental disorders, alcoholism and drug abuse: Evaluation and alternatives. *Hospital and Community Psychiatry, 35*, 452-455.

Thompson, M. (1980). *Benefit-cost analysis for program evaluation*. Newbury Park, CA: Sage.

Tufte, E. R. (1983). *The visual display of quantitative information*. Cheshire, CT: Graphics.

Veroff, J., Kulka, R., & Dourvan, E. A. (1981). *Mental health in the United States: Patterns of help-seeking from 1957-1976*. New York: Basic Books.

Wainer, H. (1984). How to display data badly. *American Statistician, 38*, 137-147.

Wang, P.C.C. (Ed.). (1978). *Graphic representation of multivariate data*. New York: Academic Press.

Warheit, G. J., & Bell, R. A. (1983). The use of the field survey to estimate mental health needs. In R. A. Bell, M. Sundel, J. F. Aponte, S. A. Murrell, & E. Lin (Eds.), *Assessing health and human service needs* (pp. 179-190). New York: Human Sciences Press.

Weiss, C. H., & Bucuvalas, M. J. (1980). *Social science research and decision making*. New York: Columbia University Press.

Wennberg, J., & Dittelsohn, A. (1973). Small area variations in health care delivery. *Science, 82,* 1102-1108.

Witkin, B. R. (1977). Need assessment kits, models and tools. *Evaluation Technology, 17*, 5-18.

Workman, K. R. (1980). *Needs assessment of married student housing: A comparison of strategies*. Unpublished doctoral dissertation, Southern Illinois University at Carbondale.

INDEX

ABOUT THE AUTHOR

Jack McKillip is Professor of Psychology at Southern Illinois University at Carbondale. His research interests include research designs for program evaluation, methodological issues in survey research, and the application of social psychological theories to health promotion planning. He has published several articles on these topics in program evaluation journals, and is consulting editor to the journal *Criminal Justice and Behavior*. He is the coauthor, with Gordon F. Pitz, of *Decision Analysis for Program Evaluation* (Sage Publications, 1984).

NOTES